CHRISTINA DODWELL

Christina Dodwell was born in 1951. Her first journey was made on horseback in 1975 at the start of three years of travelling in Africa, which she described in TRAVELS WITH FORTUNE. Other horse journeys followed, which are recounted in IN PAPUA NEW GUINEA, AN EXPLORER'S HANDBOOK and A TRAVELLER ON HORSEBACK, a journey which took her across the mountains of eastern Turkey. She has also rafted white water rapids and canoed the Yellow River in China, which she tells of in A TRAVELLER IN CHINA, and in TRAVELS WITH PEGASUS she learns to microlight in order to explore West Africa. When not travelling, Christina Dodwell lives on her farm in the Chilterns with her husband.

sceptre

Christina Dodwell

BEYOND SIBERIA

sceptre

British Library C.I.P.

A CIP catalogue record for this title is available from the British Library

ISBN 0-340-59035-1

Printed and bound in Great Britain for Hodder and Stoughton Paperbacks, a division of Hodder Headline PLC, 338 Euston Road London NW1 3BH by Cox & Wyman Ltd, Reading, Berks.

CONTENTS

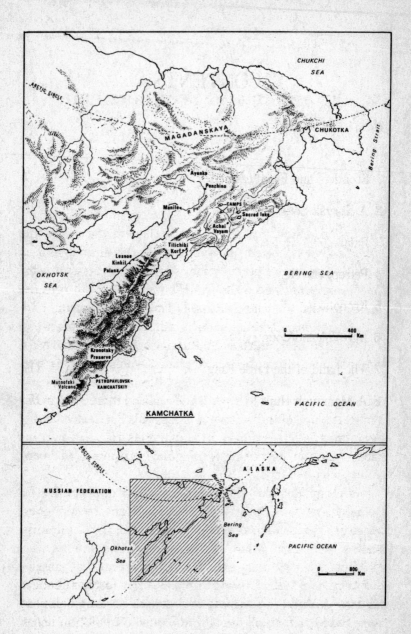

CHUKCHI
SEA

ARCTIC CIRCLE

MAGADANSKAYA

CHUKOTKA

Bering Strait

Ayanka

Penzhino

Manily

R. Penzhina

CAMPS

Sacred lake

Achai
Vayam

Tilichiki
Korf

OKHOTSK
SEA

BERING SEA

Lesnoe
Kinkil
Palana

0   400
              Km

Kronotsky
Preserve

Mutnofski
Volcano

PETROPAVLOVSK-
KAMCHATSKIY

PACIFIC OCEAN

__KAMCHATKA__

ARCTIC CIRCLE

ALASKA

Bering Strait

RUSSIAN FEDERATION

Bering
Sea

Okhotsk
Sea

PACIFIC OCEAN

0   800
              Km

1

Frontiers and Frontiersmen

The first machine to walk on the surface of the moon, the *lunakhod*, was tested in Kamchatka, the thumb-shaped peninsula beyond Siberia which stretches north-east toward the Bering Strait and a thousand kilometres south into the Pacific toward the islands Russia disputes with Japan.

To most Russians Kamchatka is still as remote as the moon and a visit there as unlikely. In Russian schools, I discovered, the back seat of the class is dubbed Kamchatka. This synonym for total alien remoteness first attracted me when I was contemplating a visit to Siberia and realised there was an area almost the size of India beyond it, Russia's Far East, a land of permafrost and volcanoes, of indigenous reindeer-herding tribes and the descendants of gulag prisoners, of bears, sables, caviar and gold.

For many decades there had been no opportunity for casual travel here for either Soviet citizens or foreigners because Kamchatka was a major test area for the Communist nuclear arms race. Many of the people I was to meet were children of the military scientists involved in that massive and crippling cold war programme. But glasnost has changed all that. A Russian shipping and general trading company were happy to furnish me with the official invitation necessary for obtaining a visa because the idea that a foreigner might tell the world about the wonders of their remote territory was for them a way to meet the uncertain future.

Continuing my research, I discovered there was not one contemporary book about Kamchatka in English. The older books in the Royal Geographical Society Library had a lot to say about the indigenous tribal people and I wanted very much to discover how that traditional side of Kamchatka life fitted into today's world.

I needed to travel for at least three months, giving me time to get to the more remote and inaccessible areas. The authorities were helpful but mystified by my interest, and horrified that I intended to travel in winter. 'Go in autumn, that's the most beautiful and easy time,' they pushed. But I don't learn much by enjoying only the good times. Even with my track record of living rough, I think they hoped I wasn't serious. But within two months my visa was ready at the Russian Consulate, all written in Russian which I couldn't yet read.

While I talked to my contacts, I read on into Kamchatka's history, reminding myself that up until the mid-nineteenth century it had not even been the boundary of Russia's vast empire. Under Peter the Great, a century before that, the navigator Vitus Bering had discovered the strait that was to take his name and explored Alaska. The first maps of America's north-west were made by Russians, but when the area did not prove to be a land as readily convertible to milk and honey as had been hoped, Tsar Alexander II sold it to President Buchanan in 1867 for less than two cents an acre. The American people called it a senseless purchase of a chest full of ice. It would be another century before they discovered what an oil-rich bargain they had acquired.

Today the reindeer-herders of northern Kamchatka still have far more in common culturally with their Inuit cousins across the Bering Strait than with a Russian administration emanating from Moscow or even from the territory's administrative centre at Petropavlovsk-Kamchatskiy in the south. I wanted to visit these scattered nomads and find out how much of their traditional lifestyle had survived the remorse-less Soviet steamroller.

But everywhere I turned in planning my trip I came back to the formidable facts of distance and terrain. From Moscow to Petropavlovsk is nine time zones, while travel within Kamchatka itself is logistically complicated by the lack of roads and the nature of its high volcanic backbone and vast feature-less tundra. The obvious way to travel would be by dog or reindeer-sled – another good reason for choosing the winter. Winter lasts seven months in Kamchatka and snow lies on the ground until June.

I arrived at the beginning of March and made my way up to Palana on the west coast of the peninsula because I had heard that the Beringei dog-sled race was due to pass through the town. As it happened, I arrived two weeks too early for that, but had the good fortune to be told of a local song and dance troupe who were soon to go on tour for ten days entertaining the reindeer-herder camps hundreds of miles apart in the tundra where the peninsula of Kamchatka joins the mainland of Russia's Far East.

If I could persuade them to take me along I would not have a better opportunity of visiting these scattered nomads and, fortunately, they agreed. We would be travelling by heli-copter in order to cover the vast distances, but afterwards and for the rest of my trip, getting about would become a bit more physical. So I filled in the time waiting for the artistes to assemble by finding out at first-hand just how cold it would be, how my clothing would stand up to the temperatures, and having a first taste of getting about as the local people do.

The moment you sit on a sled the dogs bound forward. Makar and I hurtled through Palana's outskirts, still asleep at that early hour, with lazy wisps of steam rising from small wooden houses and from leaks in the urban central heating system which pipes hot water round the streets from house to house. Through this tranquillity lurched our sled, the dogs in a frenzy, scrabbling to take every side turning and chase every cat. Makar was braking hard, leaning on the wooden pole with a sharp metal end which jabbed into the snow between sled and runner and strut.

Once clear of the town we harnessed two extra dogs, making the team up to eight. One kept jumping up affectionately trying to lick my face. Dogs here are good natured because they are important, so well treated. Leaving the snow road we followed a small track beside a frozen stream. Leafless willows looked stark and black against the snow. The stream banks were bordered with snowy sculptures, and from a small bridge dangled a mass of icicles. With the creaking of the sled, hissing of runners, and Makar's clucking and chirping commands, I began to relax. I was pleased I had decided on a winter journey. Our destination was a place an hour's drive away called Starikovski which means 'Old Man's Creek'. The old man referred to was Makar.

Another sled came towards us on the path, but fortunately it was wide enough and we slid past with a minimum of snarling among the dogs. The drivers greeted each other and the second one said, 'Well, Makar, I see you're bringing another bride.'

Makar is seventy-one years old, with a wife and seven children, but he often joked that it was about time he got married. His face was typically Koryak, dark tanned with prominent cheekbones and rather flat nose, somewhat like a North American Indian. The Koryaks, in the north-west, are Kamchatka's second-largest ethnic minority, and Palana is their main centre and territory capital.

In origin they are descended from the most ancient Palaeo-Asiatic inhabitants of North-east Asia. When European cavemen were painting bison and mammoth, people here were carving mammoth tusks into hooks and buckles. The other remnants of Palaeo-Asiatic and Palaeo-Siberian tribes now left in Kamchatka are Chukchi (the largest group, living to the north-east), Eveni (in the north), and scattered Itelmen. Later, to the south there were the Kamchadals, though old books use the word to mean Itelmen. The south used to be inhabited by the Ainu tribe, but they migrated to Japan when the Russians arrived.

It began snowing lightly, tiny daggers that sparkled in the light. It was quite cold, about −20°C. Makar was wearing clothes of reindeer skin, topped by a *kurlanka* like mine. A kurlanka is a personal tent, A-shaped, with no opening in front to let in the cold, and belted for extra warmth. It's made of reindeer skin and decorated with beads. Under it I wore three pairs of trousers, Damart, fleece, and Gore-tex weatherproof, above these more layers of Damart and fleece. I also wore two pairs of socks, gloves and mittens, balaclava, scarf and fur hat. And I was sometimes cold. Whenever I travelled people fussed over whether I was wearing enough of the right things, pulling me in and out of various hats and coats.

Three huts came into view among trees at the frozen river's edge, and dogs barked. Bits of deer fat were drying on strings outside the door, and inside we found Hilin, Makar's wife. We had arrived at Old Man's Creek. All Makar and Hilin's seven children are reindeer people and follow the traditional lifestyle. Their daughters are skilled at making Koryak clothes, and I watched Suzviy (meaning river) scraping deer-leg skin to make boots. The tight-haired leg-skin is best at withstanding damp — legs for legs. Her scraper was a straight piece of wood with a flint of blue obsidian set in it from one of Kamchatka's many active volcanoes.

Suzviy wanted me to try scraping a kurlanka skin. It wasn't easy to find the right pressure, and I worried I'd rip a hole in it. I noticed several holes in the skin already and suggested she'd been working in her sleep, but she said the holes were made by maggots from flies that lay their eggs under the deer's skin.

'It doesn't matter, we eat the maggots, and patch the holes,' and she pointed out that my kurlanka had several such holes.

It was so. Each had been neatly patched with a coin-sized scrap of skin, and some had been ingeniously turned into features with beads in sunburst patterns. Two patches on the back had tassels hanging from the centre, which are considered amulets against harm.

Typical winter clothing has outer trousers with the hair facing out and an under-pair with it facing in, very insulating and pretty ticklish. Young people, I discovered, wear the thin supple skins of young deer and old men wear the stiffer autumn skins. The skins are softened by rubbing with a mixture of dung and reindeer urine before being dyed with a decoction of the chestnut-coloured bark of alder bushes, then smoked over the fire to make them waterproof. Reindeer hairs, like those of the polar bear, are hollow to afford the animal extra insulation. The only trouble is they are very brittle, break easily and get everywhere.

Another of Hilin's daughters was making thread, using deer sinews. Hilin was left-handed as a result of a childhood accident which had, she explained, the advantage that no one asked her to make thread for them, a left-handed twist would mean the thread unravelling if used by a right-hander.

Over lunch of boiled reindeer meat, pickled wild garlic and chunks of seal fat, Hilin told me how in her youth she saw lights at night from the new Russian settlement at Palana for the first time and thought they were stars. When she saw a pig she was amazed and decided it must be a reindeer without its coat on!

In fact Russian colonisation of this end of the world began with some Cossacks during the reign of Ivan the Terrible, who gave unlimited rights to west Siberia to a powerful merchant clan named Strogonov. The Strogonovs created a mercenary force of Cossacks, only 1,600 men and three cannons, but they are written in history as the conquerors of Siberia. Though my history book was a Communist one, it said 'the Russians were greeted by the indigenous inhabitants as liberators. All the tribes recognised the authority of the Tsar.' To me that sounded unlikely, the only true bit being that the Koryaks had not put up a fight.

Makar took me ice-fishing in the afternoon, walking out on the frozen river to join three men drilling holes in the ice to drop their lines through. 'Your turn,' said one and cleared back half a metre of snow to reveal the ice. Ice slivers churn up as the drill goes in, and the work is harder as the ice grows thicker. I had to keep clearing the hole, and after I had drilled a metre deep and was nearly at water level the ice was hard as iron. When I broke through, the water surged up the hole under pressure from the weight of ice pressing on the river.

Makar went off, leaving me to fish with the men. They baited my hook with a river worm from a gritty shell, and sandpapered the fly to make it shine. The line was wound round a short piece of wood. The technique, as one man demonstrated, involved letting out fifteen metres of line slowly, then pulling it equally slowly back in, jerking it to make the lure flash. He said it is light under the ice and the current is fast. Ice froze on the line with each winding in. My hook snagged and I caught nothing.

Makar came back with a dead reindeer on his sled, saying he had no faith that I'd catch enough fish for supper, so here was some meat. Two puppies had a tug of war with the small intestine. More of Makar's children came and went, including Inna who was a member of the dance troupe with whom I was planning to travel for the next ten days.

The children piled on to a horse-sled and went off to Palana before dark, while I stayed the night at the camp with Makar and Hilin. Supper began with a bowl of blood soup, fresh and thick, but I wasn't sure about the lumps in it; gobs of blood or chopped plants? The taste was fine, and Hilin said it would make me sleep well. We sat on piles of deerskins on the raised wooden sleeping-platform which filled most of the hut.

At night I was so buried under a heap of deerskins I could hardly move, but it was very warm. It snowed all night. The temperature was −30°. Makar loaded more wood on the fire several times in the night and put the kettle on at five a.m. Other minor night events were the noisy use of the pisspot, which they had also offered me in case of need.

In the morning it was light by eight a.m. and tea was ready.

When I brushed my hair I was surprised to see so many white hairs in my brush. Of course, they were reindeer hairs, all over my clothes too, and even in my tea. For breakfast we had fish and a ladle of tart purple berries, stored in a glass jar big enough to last the winter.

The dogs were buried under the new snow and as I went out, their heads popped up through the white blanket, blinking at me in the early light.

I borrowed a pair of hunters' skis of birchwood with leather toe loops and bits of springy wire round the heels, and spent the day alone following the river's course. Makar had warned me to avoid where trees overhang the river, as there could be thin ice under the snow.

It was a glorious sunny day, the wind was fresh but not strong. The hunters' skis were shorter than alpine ones, but sealskin strips nailed on the undersides were as effective against backsliding as the commercially produced versions.

Leaving the river, I climbed a hill, and looked down on the river's course, frozen ox-bow lakes, sled tracks, fishing-holes, and trees stunted and bent over by the weather. In the hills I seemed to be walking over the tops of cedar bushes, not easy on skis and I took a few falls. The skis were useless at edging, their edges being rounded and lacking bite, and my clothes were cumbersome.

Back across the river I continued through meadows and copses, learning to glide. Before I reached the summer track I heard a sled and a man singing with the full force of his deep bass voice. A dog team of twelve came bowling around the corner, their bulky master wearing a big red fox-fur hat, and singing with all his might. The valley reverberated.

2

A Koryak Song and Dance

There were fourteen of us, all in different hats: fox, wolverine, mink, reindeer, dog, rabbit; round, flat, pillbox, and bonnet. The dance troupe consisted of four girls and four men, red-fox hat was married to reindeer hat. She was an Even from the north with flat face, wide high cheekbones and narrow eyes, he a dark-tanned Koryak. Arctic-fox hat was Taya, the best singer. Of the men, Sasha, in a Koryak fur bonnet, was the most talented, writing the words to some of their songs and setting them to old tunes. He saw me looking at his hat and passed it over for inspection. It reminded me of an old woman's mob cap, with a turned-up rim of wolf fur. Under a hat with great earflaps was Yuri, a charming young Russian whose job I hadn't sorted out; Nadya, a teacher from Tigil, a village near Palana, was aboard as my interpreter; and there was Nikolai, the President of the Koryak National Association, who had work to do with the reindeer-herders we would meet along the way.

We flew north up the coast of the Okhotsk Sea, over sea-ice cracking into plates like giant crazy paving. We were heading for Manile at the northernmost tip of the gulf. The coast was edged by cliffs and beyond them ranged low snow-clad hills, speckled with trees. There were no signs of people. The total population of Kamchatka is merely 450,000 and most of them live in the south. The north has little but tundra and reindeer.

The troupe were playing cards. They do these tours several times a year, so are blasé about flying. Yuri made the card game noisy and full of laughter. He was an outgoing romantic who said he had been raised on love songs. Nadya however had never been in a helicopter before and was white as a sheet. But she said it was less terrifying than the prospect of translating in and out of English.

After two hours' flight Manile settlement appeared, its snow streaked with coal dust around ugly concrete apart-ment buildings and a small summer harbour. We had lunch at the settlement canteen of pasta soup and cold fish with cold rice. Nadya ate only bread, afraid of the food. The girls said there were bigger dangers. Last time they came up here there was an earthquake.

Flying on north for two hours more, the troupe's first per-formance was at a tented camp on the Penzhino river. It was a lot colder here than in Palana, −35°C in the afternoon sun, and the children were wearing furry head-to-toe outfits whose hoods were complete with deers' ears, making them look like fawns.

The tent was made of reindeer skins, fur outwards on a frame of wooden poles. Our host said it could last a lifetime with careful repairs. Deerskin boots and clothing hung around the walls and we sat on a mattress of birch twigs covered with deerskins drinking tea round the wood stove while people arrived; we were twenty-three by the time the girls started making ready, putting on their headbands and kurlankas. The concert would be outside, the audience perched on a semi-circle of deer-sleds.

The first dance was called 'Rhythm of the Tundra'. Squawking like seagulls, the girls knelt and fluttered their hands behind their backs. The squawking became a song with a chorus of musical trilling as they mimed birds bathing in shallow water, growing more melodious as they dried their

16

feathers and flew, seeming to wheel in the sky. The blue sky stretched all around our flat horizon and the white of the snow beneath the girls' noiseless feet heightened the impression of open space. Yuri told me the seagull is honoured by a spring festival when they come back to land to build nests. The dance belongs to the Itelmen people, and one of the girls, who was an Itelmen, did a solo of finding her wings and learning to fly. It is actually a dance about the soul's hesitation and the need to love.

The men performed a dance showing their Koryak soul which involved a lot of leaping, stomping, and hitting a big tambourine-style drum between their legs as they sprang in the air. Their faces were stern, it was an exciting dance. The seal ballet following it had a lot of bottom-wiggling. One dance was about a hunter who was no good and another hunter who dressed as a bear and tried to frighten him as a practical joke. Real-life incidents are also remembered in song and dance, like the story of a man who went fishing and hooked himself on the lip, which happened two years ago to the troupe's accordion player.

More traditional was a fight-dance between a hunter and a wolverine, the animal's skin worn on the dancer's hand like a puppet, with realistically snapping jaws. The pair circled round each other's tracks until the hunter was distracted by a raven, a bird of great significance to the Koryak. He dropped his spear, and the wolverine attacked. A fight to the death ended with the man killing the wolverine, and taking it home for his wife to make into hats.

The audience, young and old, were enjoying themselves, my neighbour was slapping his hand into his fist. Hunting and fishing are as dominant in life as in dance. Pyotr, the musician, told me the troupe have to supplement their food supply and spend the whole of the autumn hunting, fishing and gathering berries to last through the long winter. There is no call for concert tours anyway in the autumn because the reindeer camps are too busy.

17

An extraordinary solo followed by Danil, playing a *Wanyaya* or Jew's harp to sound like a running deer and neck-singing at the same time. I was told that a man has two vocal organs, one for speaking and the other for singing which has atrophied in most people but some Koryaks still have it. The alien *hai-ya-ha* of neck-singing sounded very similar to the Jew's harp itself.

After the concert we went back into the tent, all twenty-three of us, to feast on tender boiled venison. Our host said the family would move camp the next day. Moving on was a fact of life and at this season they did so every ten days, depending on what pasture the reindeer could dig out beneath the snow. Each deer-herders' brigade looks after about a thousand head of reindeer, and usually consists of a family unit of about half a dozen. A bachelor who joined this family had later married one of two sisters, which created a bond between him and the other sister's husband described not as 'brother-in-law' but as 'man of the wife's sister is the old male-brother beyond,' and 'man of the wife's sister is on the same lake-shore a fall companion.' It meant they should fight at each other's side to the very end.

'Which is the best time of year?' I asked and they said spring when reindeer give birth. It would happen in two months' time and everyone would celebrate the event.

The helicopter came back for us at five p.m. and we scuttled aboard through clouds of fine snow as its rotor didn't stop whirling. The savage cold tore at my skin and throat. After dropping off two groups of herdsmen at their camps, Pilot Yuri invited me into the all-glass cockpit's jump seat. He wrapped my hands around two bits of frame, said, 'Hold tight,' and pointed the nose at the ground. It was an amazing sensation, falling three hundred metres in a glass ball, before we levelled out over a broad valley with winding spruce-clad islands and flat table-topped hills, all in white. The Penzhino river broadened into a lake, chunks of ice were broken and re-formed and in patches of thin ice the colour was brilliant azure blue. On the river, too, new ice made turquoise streaks in a black and white landscape.

The helicopter plunged again, and we zoomed along five metres above the river-ice, occasionally hopping over islands. A dog-sized wolverine galloped along a side channel, its long shaggy coat bouncing. We levelled out again to three hundred metres and counted moose. The flight engineer, Valery, said that a few years ago they flew many live moose by helicopter from north to south Kamchatka as part of a project to reintroduce moose to the south.

A big hill with glistening white slopes lay directly ahead. We went straight at it, and pulled into a slow steep climb, labouring up over the peak, and sharply down the other side, the nose at a hairy angle. I grabbed for safe support and wondered if the troupe were still playing cards. Nadya would be terrified. Perhaps I should ask the pilot to calm down, but I didn't and he took us ground-hugging and mountain-jumping all the way to Manile. What a show-off!

I took confidence from the fact that with eight thousand flying-hours to his credit, he knew what he was doing; but was less happy knowing how many of these helicopters were veterans of the Afghanistan War.

At supper in the Manile canteen I apologised to everyone for encouraging the aerobatics. They responded good naturedly that perhaps I'd like to fly low enough to count mice. Lisa added that Pilot Yuri had done equally bad things to them in the past, like the time he had flown up a mountain-side then turned off the engine. 'There was silence, no whirling of blades, we thought the end had come. Then he re-started the motor. But if you let him do it too often, we'll leave you behind somewhere!'

We stayed at a sort of hostel, and I shared a room with the girls. Inna, the youngest at twenty-two, was the daughter of Makar from Old Man's Creek. She said her name means star;

Lisa had forgotten her Even name. She said her grandmother had known it but she was dead. We would be visiting Lisa's home settlement the following week. There was plump Larissa whose name in Koryak is Kaychelg, meaning tender and delicate. Remembering the seal-waggle of her bottom I found it hard to think of her as fragile. Larissa grew up in Bila-gavoy, a village that was closed in 1973 when she was eleven. The villagers were divided into five groups and sent to live in other villages or collective holding-stations. Those who agreed to move had the choice of where to go. The old people who refused to move were forcibly put in new homes.

Most of the dance troupe had from the age of seven attended restricted or closed boarding-schools, which meant you were forbidden to go out. Russian was the only language allowed, their own languages were banned. They were taught Russian history and culture, and they had to get used to a totally different diet from the one they grew up with. When they went home to their tents, generally once a year for the summer holiday, many found themselves embarrassed by their families' primitive way of life and could not even understand their own language any more.

They all agreed they had hated school. This formula for incorporating the Koryak people and other minorities into Russia has not been a success. The ethnic groups are usually poor students because they do not see the relevance of what they learn. The boys are taught very little of any use to lads growing up to be reindeer-breeders, which means the skill is dying out, and what will life be like for them in the future if there are no more reindeer? Girls leave school unable to live happily in the tundra or cook their traditional foods. Yet these girls were born to be the wives of herdsmen. So who can the boys marry? The official Communist textbook view was that the small nationalities of the north were 'saved from extinction by the advent of Soviet power which put them on the road to material prosperity.' Looked at from the other end of the telescope, of course, it could be described as cultural genocide.

But there is one ray of hope and the dance group are part of it. Since perestroika there has been a revival of interest in culture and folklore and classes are being introduced to teach the children their own language. It was the troupe's own generation who suffered most. As Taya said ruefully, 'How can we relearn our culture? A native child is like a flower, you cannot pick it, then try to plant it again.'

Nadya chipped in to say how her pupils at the school in Tigil had little interest in studies but were talented in painting and traditional arts. So far on this trip Nadya was like a fish out of water. She slept in her bra, put curlers in her hair, and said she felt dirty without a bath. She had no bathroom at her home but visited her mother-in-law who did. Our dormitory beds were scarcely two foot wide and sagged dreadfully in the middle. But they had clean starched sheets and quilt covers for the eiderdowns. Thirty-two-year-old Nadya said she had never been away from home before. Her father had come from Ukraine, her mother from Russia, and Nadya's grey-green eyes and features were almost Germanic. How can a schoolmistress of a remote village be such a softie? I teased and she replied that she only went into the tundra protected by her big policeman husband. She was still very nervous about translating for me, she was afraid of helicopters, of the cold, of nature, of people, and of failing.

We made a short thirty-minute flight in the morning to a camp just south of Manile's coastal estuary, passing the cliffs where the flight engineer Valery said a mammoth had been found a few years ago. Mammoths were here before they were pushed north into extinction.

Before we could enter the Koryak tent which was the assembling point for the concert, an old woman hurried out and placed a pile of smouldering charcoal at the entrance. We each had to put a thread or tuft from our clothing on to the embers, signifying the leaving-outside of any bad influence that we might otherwise bring in.

21

Lisa told me that if people leave their tent and go to stay at another camp, they must take a little charcoal from their own fire with them in order to come back healthy. They also believe that the noises a fire makes can be interpreted. A long strong whistling sound is a message to cancel any hunting or fishing plans or you will have an accident.

It was a big tent with a second entrance-hall tent. *'Amtor, amtor,'* I said, returning their greetings. Nikolai, the Koryak National Association man gave a speech in Koryak and I listened to the flow of tones and the way the words end with clicking t, d, k sounds. We had soup and tea, and people exchanged their news.

An old man arrived. It seemed he had come from the reindeer herd several kilometres away in a very short time but was not in the least out of breath. Yuri said the man had been eating magic toadstools, the kind that give a lift and hallucinations for about three hours. Koryaks have always used toadstools, drying them to keep when the season is over. Everyone was in good spirits, lying back on the twig and skin mattress, Danil was playing his accordion, softly fingering wistful bits of tunes, sometimes one or two girls hummed a descant. When anyone stood up, dust and reindeer hairs flew and wafted in the air. More herdsmen arrived, tucking their shotguns out of the raw cold under the rugs of their sleds.

The concert when it began wasn't the easiest because of frequent interruptions; dogs barked as reindeer walked through the camp, Toadstool Man commented on the dancing, another old man had a faulty hearing-aid which made loud bip, bip, bip noises, and a woman came in with a sack and started pulling out fur clothes for the man beside me. The garments didn't seem to please him and he made her empty the whole bag on the floor. The dancers kept tripping over a log that held in the twig mattress. Then they did a sketch about toadstools.

In it a couple of men are making a journey on foot, they grow tired, have a rest, find toadstools and the elder man eats them. The younger man is afraid to because toadstools are only used by the over-forties. They continue the journey, treading tight circles in the tent, until they see a stick across their path. To the hallucinating elder it is a tree trunk so large he struggles to climb over it. At a small gulley he recoils in horror, seeing a wide river, and jabbers at his friend, 'I can't swim.' His friend agrees to help him across, carrying him on his back. The story ends with the old man going home and the young one finding a glade of toadstools to pick for his grandmother.

Yuri came up with the idea that our Father Christmas who drives a reindeer sled through the sky, wearing the red and white colours of the toadstool, might have originally been a hallucination.

At the troupe's last number, Mr Toadstool joined in and wouldn't stop dancing, beating a drum at the same time, lost in his magic world. We all tried clapping to stop him and the musicians put down their instruments, but he was oblivious. So the group joined in for an encore, and finally it ended.

The sun was setting, but there was no sign of the helicopter, so after a supper of reindeer stew and strips of dried fish, we all went outside to look for a helicopter speck in the sky. The sunset was rosy. A score of reindeer, the domestic draught deer that pull sleds, ambled into the camp. They were smaller than I had expected, much smaller than cattle. Several had already shed their antlers, and without horns they had rather ugly long faces with fat noses.

Our host's family were well-established sled-makers and about twenty were ranged in line on the snow, made of smooth polished birchwood which is the hardest and most supple wood in this region. The joints were rounded and lashed with seal thongs, which makes them flexible. Nailed joints would snap, jolting along in such cold.

As with cars, there are different kinds of sled to suit your station in life. The smallest is a narrow lightweight racing-sled, 250 centimetres long, though almost half the length is the bow of the runners which curves gracefully up and back to form the seat sides, giving springy suspension. A series of arches between runners and seat hold the whole thing together. There is a broader and longer sled for the family, with wide runners for their feet to rest on, a type with sides for carrying big and awkward loads, and a mother and child sled with built-in basket. You pack the child in furs and the basket is tall enough to stop the child climbing out. When I asked the price of a sled they couldn't tell me, since they barter them for goods and favours.

Darkness fell with no sign of our helicopter, so we retired to the tent and some old women began critically examining the embroidery and beadwork on the dancing-girls' costumes to be sure that they had followed tradition. I sat beside the woman who had brought the sack of clothes, trying on a decorated headband with long tassels of beads hanging from it. She said beads come from Alaska in exchange for furs, and it only takes a day to go on the sea-ice across the Bering Strait from Chukotka to Alaska, which makes you realise just how arbitary this political border of east and west is. After all, Alaska was sold to the United States as recently at 1867, and thirty thousand years before, a land bridge would have joined the continents.

It was night when finally the helicopter arrived. We clambered aboard with two dogs and some extra Koryaks. I went to the back and found space beside a large dead wolf. Its handsome thick creamy fur was tinged black, its mouth set in a snarl that showed inch-long canines. Some Koryaks had shot it when it attacked their deer herd. I hoped it was fully dead. All through the flight, as Anatoly's creamy dog-fur hat bobbed about I kept thinking the wolf was moving.

Pilot Yuri was on top form. I sat on the auto-pilot box in the nose and we flew north along the coast of the Okhotsk Sea past icebergs, and three tall sea stacks. Yuri said he had once landed his helicopter on the tallest, but there had not been enough space for him to set foot. We passed some islands, with bird cliffs where in summer they sometimes landed to gather eggs of kittiwakes, eider, geese, sea-ducks, puffins (horned and tufted), cormorants, auks, and black guillemots with scarlet legs. He said the difference between high and low tides here was a staggering fourteen metres.

We were heading for Yurt Mekino, on the Mekino River, and arrived in time for breakfast of reindeer and *aladyr* (my favourite bread-like things). I said we don't have these in England, and Larissa asked how can you live without them. I said indeed how can we live without them.

Nadya took me to a hut where two elderly Koryak women showed us their collection of protective family totems, which were hanging in bunches from a pole alongside shotguns and antlers. The oldest woman unhooked them and spread them out on a deerskin. There were four flat wooden figures with the idea of legs and heads. The largest was half a metre tall, and over one hundred years old. She explained they were dirty because people feed them at festivals, smearing them with reindeer fat. Suddenly, she began bashing two of them together, saying that if a family is afflicted with bad luck, like the deer being ill, the women punish the totems for not doing their work.

These totems are not gods; Koryaks believe the world is ordained by a Supreme Being who sends glut or famine but has no interest in their consequence. Men are left to their own ideas of how to protect themselves from harm, diseases and evil spirits. This is where the totems come in. Wealthy folk have big ones, and a rich relation may let his family totem go to visit and help out a poor relation until his luck changes.

Small stones found in a deer's stomach were important in the rituals connected with curing sickness and were used whenever a shaman was called. Shamans are now a thing of the past, hunted out and 'dissuaded' under Russian rule. I often asked people about them, and learned plenty about their past but nothing of the present. Koryaks had the simplest form of shaman religion, made up of superstition, magic and animism. It was a way of coming to terms with the outer world, and their own inner being. A shaman's regular daily duties included helping the sick, finding lost reindeer, and giving advice. They used a drum, like the troupe's musicians, for their dancing and to invoke and communicate with the spirit world. Apart from informal family shamans, there were big-name professionals who ran the ceremonials on special occasions. To be among these one needed a supernatural gift, sometimes it was hereditary. But to reach the top required more than mere showmanship. One young shaman who could do all the tricks, like swallowing a stick, stabbing himself with a knife, eating red-hot coals, and being in different places at the same time, still was not considered first-class; whereas an inspired old woman, who did not perform all these tricks, was held in great esteem and fame.

Some of the best shamans were nervous unstable people, given to fits, alternating with complete exhaustion. They could lie motionless for two or three days without food or drink. I read about a young man of twenty who began seeing and hearing things others did not. For six years he struggled with himself, and kept it secret, as he was afraid people would make fun of him. At last he became so ill he was on the verge of death; but when he started to act as a shaman he grew better. He frequently had his shamanistic objects confiscated and burned for, under Soviet rule, all shamans' arts and artifacts were banned, but he kept practising his art because he found he became ill again if he didn't. Gradually, however, shamans faded away under Communism. Only the drums were left – the most important shaman object throughout Kamchatka, Siberia and among the American Eskimos.

Before the concert started two musicians, Anatoly and Fedya, wound up a *vertushka*, a slice of birchwood spinning on a long walrus-hide rope which they pulled humming and buzzing between them in what became almost a tug-of-war to break the rope. If it is not broken on the day it is made, they

26

must keep going the next day until it does break. The result, whenever it is achieved, is two lengths of super-supple high-quality thong that may last a lifetime.

The buzzing birchwood disk was part of the Hololo dance, everyone's favourite, symbolising the three- or four-day festival after the surplus deer are slaughtered for meat and skins when the herd comes home at the end of the year.

Larissa picked up two wooden totems which were part of the troupe's equipment, twirling and kneeling to make them dance behind her back. Then she passed them to Danil who did the same. Totems can take a person's spirit up through the Hololo dance until the dancer reaches ecstasy. I pointed out that one of theirs had lost its head, but Danil said it didn't matter in the least.

The fumes of kerosene leaking from a petrol drum got steadily worse in the flight on to Ayanka and my head throbbed. The drum had been full on take-off and the altitude made the kerosene expand; if it hadn't leaked it might have exploded instead. Though we opened the portholes, we couldn't wait to scramble down the ladder when we landed at Ayanka, near some larch trees on a vast plain.

We were further north now, far above the peninsula in the great wastes of the mainland, and the air temperature was dropping fast, already $-40°C$ according to my travelling thermometer, though we were not within the Arctic Circle. The coldest place in the world is not at the North Pole. In fact it is about 2,500 kilometres to the south, at Yakutia in eastern Siberia, where temperatures of $-70°C$ are normal in winter. A problem of big minus temperatures is that plastic boot soles snap, rubber shatters like glass, metal becomes brittle, and the fillings in your teeth fall out. Building on permafrost poses another set of problems, so houses are built above the ground on short piles, leaving air space underneath. In Kamchatka they are not higher than necessary because of the earthquake hazard.

A *buran* (the Russian answer to a skidoo) came out to meet us towing a sled, and as many as could fit climbed aboard for a ride to the administrative office, where the clerk stamped our papers and directed us to the only hotel. The hotel office said the men could stay but not the women, since there was no proper heating and no money to install any. This chivalrous gesture consigned the women to a fairly spartan hostel by the primary school. The hot-water tap was attached to the radiator, centrally heated on the pipe that went all round the settlement from house to house. For cold water we had a pump with a handle you had to crank for some time before murky water came out.

We went to the village canteen for some good home cooking, where I caused a stir because I was the first foreigner to visit Ayanka, and crowds came to look at me, which made me sorry I was not more remarkable for them, with three legs and blue or green skin. Later two little girls from the primary school took me to meet their Uncle Semgon, a Koryak reindeer-herder who had lived in this region for all his seventy years. Ayanka settlement was established in the 1940s though the Koryaks have camped here seasonally since time began. Its initial convenience was as a trading post for the exchange of inland and maritime goods. Later, the nearby estuary made it possible for Russians to bring goods by dinghy in summer. In the early colonial days they had pulled the boats by shoulder straps, taking two weeks from the coast. In winter they could use reindeer-sleds on the frozen rivers.

Semgon said his family had always been poor, so the impact of reindeer collectivisation had made little difference to him. Semgon had worked hard and become a Hero of Socialist Labour, as master in the reindeer brigade, and received a medal for it. His pension of twenty-four roubles (24p) a month was now enough to buy some sugar and daily bread, nothing more. But his motto in life was that the less one has the less one needs. Even in autumn, when all the bushes in the tundra are laden with berries, you should not take more than you need. Don't pick things just because they are there, leave some berries on every bush for birds and other animals.

Some neighbours turned up to look at me. Yuri, who was with us, said a girlfriend of his once went with a PR mission to America and people there all gathered to gawp at her, too. She said she felt like a zoo animal on show. I was more used to it, though sometimes I felt like a giant, being so much taller than the average Koryak.

In the canteen for supper I sat beside Nikolai, the President of the Koryak National Association, who had been speaking to the herdsmen en route about changes in state farm operation. He explained that all large-scale farming and fishing was until now state-run. The state used to buy nearly all the fish and reindeer meat of Kamchatka at controlled prices.

The Koryak National Association was created two years ago to protect the rights of indigenous people, Koryak and others, specifically their rights to hunt sea mammals and all wild animals, go fishing, and to herd reindeer. The purpose was to build up their own economy. But this will never flourish until they have the facilities to manufacture things themselves in their place of origin. Joint ventures with the western world seem the only way of funding this, but since Kamchatka has no form of banking guarantees, it is unlikely to attract investment. Nikolai said they had put forward a lot of different proposals to central government in Moscow, and had recently signed a Federated Treaty. They were now waiting to see what happened and he was guardedly optimistic.

We waited for the helicopter to warm up. The coldest it can fly in is $-55°$, so we should just be all right, the pilot told us. The sun had a halo, almost a rainbow, which Yuri said was ice crystals, an icebow, a phenomenon that only happens below $-50°$. At this temperature your breath can freeze as you exhale, forming tiny crystals which drop to the ground making a sound that Siberians call 'the whispering of stars'.

*

In the helicopter to Verpenjena we gave a lift to six herdsmen together with their children, baskets, bundles of skins, and some dogs. One of the children, a four-year-old toddler dressed in fur jumpsuit with white ears on the hood, was also called Christina. I asked how she came by the name and her mother said it was her grandmother's.

With the helicopter so crowded the pilot offered me the seat beside him. We crossed the plain away from the estuary, and rose into a series of jagged snowy hills. Twenty kilometres later we came to a broad river valley, studded with islands and mudflats, and washed-up piles of tree trunks covered in snow. The river wound beneath our straight line, and you could see where everyone had been, ice-fishermen, hunters and their prey, from their tracks in the snow. Tracing a set of large prints I suddenly found they led to the hooves of a moose running through the snow, across the open river and swerving into the bare woods to escape our helicopter. Pilot Yuri pointed to another moose, also running from the helicopter's noise, bounding in deep drifts up to his haunches.

Verpenjena was three deserted huts. However, my companions quickly made themselves at home, chopped wood and got the stove lit before the audience of nine arrived.

Nikolai made his speech, in Russian this time, so Nadya translated. He explained that he had no money to pay the herders' wages and that there would be no money next pay-day either. He spoke about rising prices and costs. The administration simply had no cash.

The people listened calmly as he told them there was a special hardship fund for orphans and others in real need. For the future, he talked of recent plans for reorganising the state farms so that deer are rented by private individuals or collectives. Faces looked puzzled as he went on to try explaining the concept of private enterprise. He suggested they could also supply young antler velvet (*pantui*) for making the medicine pantocrin which is used in cardio-vascular treatment. But of course Kamchatka has no facilities for manufacturing this itself and would have to sell the raw material to Japanese pharmaceutical companies for them to make the profit not the reindeer herders. Slowly, questions came as serious faces tried to grasp what it all meant in real terms. They asked what had happened to their usual allocation of tents, boots and clothing which the administration no longer had funds to provide for them. Even if they had had the money to buy their own equipment, the only things in the shops now were useless electrical goods like irons and video machines. Rather desperately, Nikolai promised a special commission from Petropavlovsk would come and solve all their problems. Who did he think he was kidding, they replied. Every year they heard promises that had never been kept.

Under the new system, a family could rent up to a thousand reindeer from the state, making a contract to herd them with a collective farm. The scheme had been in operation for three months but I was told no one had yet applied. They had no spare cash and were wary of taking initiative. If they did not lose any reindeer during a year, Nikolai ploughed on, the calves would belong to the family. Some families, he claimed, were already building up their herds, having been given reindeer as rewards from the state for hard work in the past. Of the men present, one had twenty, another thirty, and the third had fifty reindeer. But there's an economically viable number which is at least a thousand, and you must have a large enough family to care for that. Also herds of less than five hundred tend to run off and join larger herds, which was why Nikolai was urging families to join together to build up private herds. The speech left me very confused. The Koryaks took the whole thing more calmly than the one Russian herdsman, who told me he had spent seven years in the tundra, had nine deer to his name, and knew that as a Russian in Koryak territory he has less rights than anybody.

But now the dance troupe were tuning up. The highlight of their concert was a brilliant little sketch about how the administration helps the deer-herders by flying in doctors,

31

barbers and traders. The doctor has no medicine, and the barber only has time to shave half a head because the helicopter is waiting impatiently. The sketch even included a Nikolai figure who explained news and politics by flashing a newspaper past their eyes; while the trader exchanges their valuable deer products for useless goods: an electric stove, an iron, one boot, and bottles of cologne – all at extortionate prices. It was a sketch the troupe did at every camp and it always made the herdsmen laugh, they found it so true to life.

When we left to return to Ayanka we loaded the helicopter with frozen blocks of meat, like the trader in the sketch. I was just settling down in my seat when Yuri invited me to try my hand at flying the helicopter. I had told him a little about my flying adventures by microlight in West Africa and was glad I could remember some of the basics, as my lesson proceeded in Russian. I moved the joystick gingerly. The helicopter was sensitive enough and, like a ship, it continued to respond for some time after the command. Over mountains I got into a long oscillation pattern of pitching slowly, overcorrecting and trying to counteract it. Mountain turbulence hardly affected the machine, as it was stabilised by its own weight and its stabilising unit, unlike my microlight which had bounced around terribly. It was exhilarating to be flying again, but as Ayanka came into sight I mentioned that my landings were always abysmal and let Yuri take control again.

We were all starving and, on landing, mobbed the café for bowls of spuds and meat. Then the girls got ready for an evening performance at 'the Club', a centre for home-made entertainment and cultural interest. Was there any in Ayanka, population, I would guess, two hundred? I could not imagine poetry readings. Then I met the new cultural director, a young man in his early twenties who had arrived only the previous week. I asked if people were welcoming. He said they were friendly when they drank vodka with him but otherwise hardly noticed him. There was an absurd moment when as the girls sang on stage and the musicians beat their drums, he tugged Nadya and me into an anteroom, turned on the TV, pulled out a guitar and, oblivious to both TV and the concert, started to sing violent rock songs. He said he was here because he earned twice the salary he would elsewhere, three thousand roubles, or three hundred dollars a month, with no overheads. He wanted to save up to visit England and meet famous rock groups. I hoped he would mellow enough to enjoy the Koryak culture.

I could hear the Raven Dance starting and, not wanting to miss it, we slid back into the audience. Two men were on stage strutting and cawing in perfect imitation of the ravens I had become used to seeing in flocks of hundreds at every settlement. These two found a dead fish and both grabbed at it with their beaks, trying to pull it away from the other. Their movements to and fro as each tried to devour the fish were, like other acts, an odd theatrical ballet, performed with such grace and enthusiasm that we who had seen it all before were entranced every time.

No Koryak harms the ravens, believing that if you kill or disturb them you will be punished. If a raven caws in the night, bad luck is coming. Big Raven, the messenger of the Supreme Being who created everything, was sent to earth to bring people out of chaos, to put right the disorder of human life. In the time that Big Raven lived in this world, the evil spirits or *kalau* were visible to men and took grotesque shapes, like dogs with human heads. They could infiltrate men's homes through the fire in the hearth.

There is no generic name for good spirits, and the natural enemies of the kalau are Big Raven and his children. After the time of Big Raven, the kalau became invisible to men, although shamans could still see them. Some accounts say Big Raven and his family were turned into stone, others say they left the Koryaks and went to the Chukchi. In a cliff on the

33

coast near Manile is a sacred place where Big Raven's home once stood.

In all the Big Raven legends people here seem especially to relish his more scurrilous adventures and his wily ways. The dance on stage was now depicting the tale of an old man who offered his daughter in marriage to Big Raven in exchange for the bird making a long journey. The father gave the bird a bag of food for the road. Big Raven went up a hill, ate all the food, and jumped up and down until his feet were blistered. Then he lay and slept for days before returning to claim his bride. For all that, Big Raven is revered like a god but if a raven flies into a Koryak house, it is a bad omen, calling for a decent sacrifice.

The helicopter next morning filled up with Koryaks with important reasons to travel, and I was surprised to hear Nadya translate 'We are packed like sardines in a can,' never having thought it could be a Russian expression, too. I had also heard the card-players saying 'Lucky in cards, unlucky in love,' and there are Russian proverbs about making hay while the sun shines, and being a dog in a manger, as well as superstitions about a black cat crossing your path. Nadya was losing her fear of flying and settled down to doze while the group played cards and made jokes to her about keeping awake or they would send me into the pilot's seat so they could walk on the cabin sides and ceiling again.

We dropped the troupe and Nadya at a camp of skin tents and I was given the pilot's seat as we flew on to round up more audience from other camps scattered across the vast emptiness. When the helicopter was empty it was harder to fly. Yuri tried to teach me to land. At touchdown you have to keep lifting the machine up and down several times so the tyres do not freeze in.

Another day a Russian woman doctor from one of the settlements came with us, taking the opportunity to see some of her former patients in the two or three camps we would visit. The Koryaks stay perfectly healthy in the tundra but succumb to infections and poor hygiene as soon as they spend time in a settlement. Vodka is a separate problem. The people of the tundra have no tolerance for it because their traditional diet has no sugar intake. If you get your high from toadstools, you can't cope with alcohol.

We flew up the Penzhino river, saw two wolves, and stopped at a tent to pick up a herdsman to show us the way to the first camp.

While Nikolai gave his 'I cannot pay you' speech in a skin tent which smelled as if the skins were poorly cured, the doctor, a group of women and I went into a huddle and discussed women's secrets. For contraceptives some Koryaks use pizhmah, a soft yellow flower with umbelliferous heads, feathery leaves, and a distinctive smell. They make tea of it daily to prevent pregnancy, and also use the flowers or juice to rub on their skin as mosquito repellent.

Our host's daughter was due to be married, so I asked about traditional Koryak weddings. The bride goes alone into a tent and her relatives line up outside, making a corridor along which the bridegroom has to walk, while the bride's family beat him with fists and sticks. If they don't like him they sometimes try to kill him! The sixteenth-century Russian explorer, Krasheninnikov, recorded that if the suitor was unwelcome they scratched his face and dragged him by the hair. His victory was seldom quick. Sometimes getting married could take a year as, after each attempt, the prospective bridegroom needed time to recover from his wounds. One hapless would-be bridegroom tried for seven years to win his chosen woman, ending up instead a total cripple.

Inna said that if the girl loves the man she asks her family not to hurt him too much. When groom reaches his bride he tears off her clothes, because to strip the bride naked constitutes the ceremony of marriage. No bride price is paid, but presents are usually made to the bridegroom's family which, considering what mischief may have been done to the poor fellow, is not totally unreasonable.

But Koryaks are basically romantic, and Lisa told me a love song in which a mother advises her son: 'Don't be afraid to say words of love. Think of the man who loved a woman but never told her so. He told her she was the best in the world but he never said, I love you. And when he was old his heart was empty because he hadn't found the words of love. The woman had married someone else.'

The dance girls left us to go and decorate themselves for the concert, and I noticed that beneath her bulky clothes Larissa was pregnant. The doctor said that Koryak women's pregnancies seldom go for nine months, the babies usually being born after seven, and women try to remain as energetic as possible during pregnancy in order to pass this quality on to the unborn child. A pregnant woman finding stones or lumps of earth in her path should kick them away, symbolising the removal of obstruction at childbirth, and she must never turn back after setting out somewhere, otherwise the delivery will be checked in the middle. It is taboo for her to eat reindeer fat because it could thicken or 'freeze' in the stomach, and fasten the child to the inside of the womb. Koryak women are very stoical during childbirth and never cry out. I had read that if they wished to get pregnant they ate spiders, but someone else said this was nonsense as spiders are sacred and may not be eaten.

Among the maritime Koryak there used to be a system of group marriage, where up to ten couples, usually of the same family, but excluding brothers, had rights to each others' spouses as they visited different camps. The Chukchi had a similar arrangement and when the first Russian traders arrived they were offered a Chukchi wife for the night, the host having first covered the sleeping-place with beaver, fox, and marten furs, numerous enough to match the value of the presents of iron, kettles and tobacco brought by the trader. This custom no longer exists but vestiges of it can be seen in the fact that today when the eldest brother dies, the next is expected to marry the widow and look after the family. If he is already married, a younger brother is nominated, or a younger cousin or nephew. If the woman is much older, the young husband is allowed to invite a young woman to live with him as second wife. Among the Itelmen there used to be a rule that before remarrying, the widow must have sex with someone else, preferably a stranger, to cleanse her for marriage. If the woman was old she had difficulty finding a volunteer, but Krasheninnikov said that after the Cossacks arrived they were pleased to help.

Young Larissa was dancing, wiggling her ass and squawking sexily, in a raunchy dance about a girl deciding which of two men she would marry.

I asked the woman beside me if it is true that Koryak men are appallingly jealous. I had read that married women make themselves as repulsive-looking as possible, with uncombed hair, unwashed feet and hands, and worn-out clothing, expressly to avoid arousing jealousy. Unfortunately, the woman I asked was, I now noticed, particularly unkempt, and bulbously fat with a squint in both eyes. She hotly denied that her husband was jealous. Perhaps he had no reason to be. She added for good measure that of course people didn't wash much in winter, and their clothes were worn out because they couldn't get new ones.

The helicopter turned up to collect us halfway through the concert, which had started late because Nikolai had spent double the normal time on his speech. So the last dances were condensed, stressing the punchlines, and the scene of the helicopter visit bringing useless gifts had people laughing so hard they wiped tears from their cheeks.

If Nikolai could have paid them, the herdsmen would earn two thousand roubles per month, a good salary compared to other state farm workers. Even Yuri the pilot only earned six thousand roubles a month, which seems absurd for one of Kamchatka's most experienced pilots. Top doctors, dentists and miners could earn eight thousand roubles. Nadya, as a teacher, earned five thousand because she had a degree and worked extra hours. She said it was all very well to have pay rises but they did not keep pace with inflation. In the last year salaries had increased threefold, and prices tenfold. Yuri called money 'sweet-wrappings' because it was so colourful and valueless.

The helicopter crew went away to refuel while we stayed on for lunch. I jarred my teeth biting on a piece of bone by mistake. I knew I must be careful not to break any teeth in Kamchatka or I would be patched up with metal ones like everyone else. The doctor said that children's teeth are not strong because of lack of vitamins, though they are helped by wild garlic and half-cooked meat, and blood soup which helps prevent decay. The traditional form of toothpaste is called 'the tears of the tree', a sap which you warm with a match until it drops in tears into a bowl of water you cook on the fire. Later you chew a small piece of it. It tasted peppery-hot and resinous.

From camp A to camp B we flew over a great flat plain, dappled by hooves where reindeer herds had been grazing. This time the girls began loudly clearing their throats as a hint when Nikolai's speech looked set to overrun. I was engrossed in learning to make a dish from the contents of reindeer's intestines mixed with blood. It is left for some days to go sour, then hung on a rack outside to freeze. When you bring it in and melt it, it's like Italian cheese, though rather bitter to taste. I asked if people use reindeer's milk at all, and they said not often, it's so fatty. Another dish was made by souring or rotting the inside of fish heads cut in half and covered in fresh caviar. You put it all in a glass jar and make a warm hole where it stays until it goes off, which is when it is ready for eating.

At Saoundra that night the hostel was too full for all of us but a second guesthouse was found. Why, I wondered, did this place exist at all, much less have two hostels. It was smaller than my home village. At the crossroads some children had built an ice-fortress, and not far away stood a small snowman, one of very few that I'd seen. Nadya said it's not a snowman, but a *sneknaya-baba*, which means snow-woman.

Lisa caught a cold and passed it to each one of us and probably many of the herdspeople as well who are susceptible to bugs delivered by helicopter. For a day I felt terrible, too thick-headed to think, with a streaming nose. My supply of loo paper was limited. When packing for Kamchatka I had included a hundred rolls of film but only three loo rolls. I was a miserable soul all day, barely interested in anything, not even in flying, though I did pay attention when we flew past a shaman mountain.

Shaman mountains are sacred. This one near Slaoutna is revered because ancient rafts of wood, now petrified, are reputed to lie near the summit, Kamchatka's strand in the universal legend of a great flood. Nobody knows who built the rafts but they are said to be a catamaran design of two logs with cross-pieces, about four metres long. Several mountains in northern Kamchatka are supposed to bear the remains of rafts. Unfortunately, the only one we flew over was covered in snow and we could make out nothing.

We landed in Oklan for the night. For disembarking we had changed our tactics. We no longer ran from the helicopter, to receive the full blast of icy whirling snow; if you wait cowering under the blades it is less windy. We watched the helicopter ascend above us, then moved away. The village generator was broken but Yuri got it going. There was no hotel or guesthouse, so we split up between several families. This was where Lisa was born and grew up, so she knew everyone.

Despite the coal dust sullying the snow and turning even the dogs grey, Oklan was an attractive place. Its reason for existence was gold mining. Each small wooden house was set in an open space, some with fenced gardens. It still amused me to be able to step over the top few visible inches of fences which would only become effective barriers after the spring thaw. After meeting Lisa's extensive family we all went to the shop. Every settlement has one and all the troupe had visited most of them but I hadn't paid much attention because I loathe shopping, I had none of the coupons needed for purchases from state shops, and there was nothing I conceivably wanted on the half-empty shelves. Deficit was the word the Russians used to explain the space. There is a deficit of everything.

'How can you make or repair your children's clothes if you can't buy a needle?' demanded Lisa.

'For a whole year our town's shops didn't have any toothbrushes,' Larissa put in, adding, 'How would you feel if you could only buy one pair of knickers in a year?'

Oklan's shop had three dresses, some boys' trousers, plastic flowers, cheese graters, soap, kitchen mops, two types of tap, one plumbing joint, one vehicle headlight, various garden tools, a volley ball, cross-country skis, welly boots, and ice skates. Anything I could have done with Yuri said was no good and old-fashioned. But my companions were buying like it was Christmas sales time. Converting the rouble prices in my head, I found the skis were one dollar fifty and the skates eighty cents. I kept thinking I must be reading the prices wrong. The girls were buying fish hooks, pliers and rasps, and dress trimmings, while the men were choosing zips and mulling over the colours of buttons. Danil bought reels of electric flex to wire his home and Pyotr a sack of plastic sheeting to patch his greenhouse.

Nadya, Yuri and I had supper with some friends of Lisa's who had a frozen dead wolf lying in front of their fire. It was curled up just like a large sleeping dog. Our host, Valodya, explained he had been on his way back from fishing and had found two young wolves both dead. He deduced one had caught a wolverine and the other had fought for the meal.

40

Both had died of injuries. He gave one carcass to friends and brought the other home so his wife could make hats from the fur. She was good at hats. The last she made was of white Leibit swans-down, a protected species according to Russia's Red Book which registers such things. It lives in the tundra in summer. But a dead Leibit swan is a free hat.

The wolf's body would take several days to thaw. Its fur was darker than the last wolf I saw and Valodya said that was because it was a young one. I asked if the meat would be used but he said it usually smells so bad even the cat would not eat it.

Wolves are famous for their cunning and Volodya told me how they creep into camps and pretend to be dogs to be given food, how they hide camouflaged against rocks when they're hunted, and hypnotise their prey with their strange eyes. A Koryak story tells of a wolf pack that drove a reindeer herd into a narrow defile leading to a steep slope. Then half the wolf pack harryed the deer on to the lower slope, while the other half ran in line across the upper slope to crack the snow and cause an avalanche. The deer were buried and frozen. As the snow gradually melted the layers of carcasses became exposed, and the wolves had a supply of meat that lasted all winter.

Valodya taught dancing to school children, traditional Koryak dancing as well as ballet, and his wife cooked for the school boarders. They played cassettes of Koryak music as we talked after supper. The beat was like a railway train on loose tracks and I swayed sleepily.

From Oklan we flew up a valley into hills, all wound around with streams that would rush with water when the snow melted, over them and down to another great plain, totally uninhabited. I asked Pilot Yuri if he had ever broken down.

'Oh yes, many times we've had to sleep out, even in winter. The helicopter is equipped with sleeping bags, food for three days, everything but a stewardess.'

He told me a cautionary tale about someone who had tried to apply mosquito repellent at one of these enforced overnight stops and had covered his face with latex glue by mistake because the labels had worn off the tubes.

In the morning his companions looked at him in horror. What they saw was the wrinkled and wizened face of a hundred-year-old man. When the rescue helicopter finally arrived he had to be rushed straight to hospital and cleaned with spirit.

I would be sad to say goodbye to Pilot Yuri, but today was his last day with us. He was due for a holiday and would be replaced by another pilot that evening. We paused for five minutes at the village where Danil had grown up, then flew on to a group of four huts called, unromantically, Central Base. This was a base for reindeer brigades and my first chance to have a close look at the most versatile creature of the far north, the tundra's answer to the camel.

When Yuri, Nadya and I opted to spend a day minding a reindeer herd, we expected one of the herdsmen to stick around, but as soon as we arrived they all jumped into the helicopter and said they were going to the concert. Make yourselves at home, they said. Some racing sleds were parked outside the tent, and a stack of ice blocks as stored water. Wooden-plank skis and walrus webbed snowshoes were stacked upright in wigwam shapes to prevent them being lost under new snow.

Inside their tent we found the fire burning and kettle warm. We also found some lassos of twisted walrus-hide that tapered towards the end and had a running loop of filed metal to give weight to the noose. Yuri taught me how to coil one, then we stuck an antler in the snow and practised. The lasso was eighteen metres long. After a few throws we had both achieved near-misses.

The herd was grazing not far away and when we walked

towards them the majority, being wild, backed off but several draught reindeer came to greet us, rubbing their snow-caked noses on our hands, ice-balls hanging on the whiskers around their lips. We turned the rest of the herd back but they kept going and invaded the camp where two discovered an almost empty bag of salt and wouldn't back off. Nadya, who had spent the first hour cowering behind us saying she was frightened of cows, stopped fussing and was put to guard the salt, flapping her arms when the reindeer came within reach. I only managed to take a quick picture of it before my camera froze up.

The herd milled around, bells jingling. Very few had horns, having either shed them or had them removed for the pantui. Their hooves, split like cattle feet, are ideal for snow since the underside is slightly indented and the whole foot, including a double nail on the fetlock, spreads out on the snow to give support. At each pace their fore and back toes strike each other making a clicking noise as they walk. To call each other they bleat with a strange throaty *urg urg*. Like sheep, reindeer herd together and follow certain old does as their leaders. There was little we needed to do unless the herd split up or were threatened by wolves.

Nadya prepared lunch and Yuri talked about the idea of collectives. He said that central Russian peasants were starved into collectivisation. Peasants had been the landowners, an idea unacceptable to Communism. Hunger was the punishment for not letting go. During the twenty-five years of Stalin's repressions an estimated fifty million people died, a hard figure to accept but it is believed to be true.

Gentle Yuri had been captain of a Communist Youth Group. 'We all wore red scarves and had to quote lines from Lenin in every essay.'

It was militant and military Communism. People were told they were surrounded by enemies; the country was turned into a military camp. There was no such thing as unemployment because the army soaked up all the surplus manpower.

To keep such an army occupied, Russia needed to develop her foes.

'We were taught to feel threatened by you Westerners, and sorry for you, for your problems of unemployment, high prices and taxation.'

They believed they had the best living conditions in the world. Where did it go wrong? People simply say they were mistaken by propaganda.

'The whole thing was based on a lie, telling us that in five years it would be better. Perestroika was the breaking of the bubble, or laid on to soften the shock of the bubble bursting. When Gorbachev knew that Communism was dead and the Party about to collapse, he brought in fresh promises and used valuable foreign-exchange resources to fund the plans. We don't love Gorby any more. We don't love Yeltsin now either. He said no taxes and we called him a hero, then he introduced thirty per cent tax on all goods.'

Nadya summed it up: 'A few years ago we thought things were bad, but now they're worse. We wonder what tomorrow holds, the future is a mystery. By exposing our heroes as villains we've lost the past we believed in. So we have no past, and now we've no future either. Our national characteristic is patience, but maybe seventy years is enough.'

In Talovka we stayed in the pilots' guesthouse. I felt we had been there before because the layout was identical to the one in the previous settlement. We had come to visit a state farm for reindeer-breeding, and in the morning I met the director in his office. This farm which is one of eleven in the Koryak Autonomous Region, stretches from near Manile to the east coast in a narrow belt right across the neck of Kamchatka peninsula, and consists of 14,500 head of reindeer in six herds, each with its own migration route. Herds spend winter in the west side and in late May begin a two months' migration to the east coast where the mosquitoes are fewer and the deer drink seawater to improve their condition.

Remembering Nikolai's speech about not being able to pay his deer-herders, I asked about the problems. The Director threw his hands in the air.

'If we could find anyone to buy our venison, we could pay our workers. Where can we sell fresh deer meat? We will slaughter four thousand deer this year, and may end up almost having to throw it away. In the past the state bought our meat but now they have cut their order by half because of prohibitive transport costs. Yet state law requires our stocks must remain level.

'There are no canning or refrigeration facilities here, no economical way to treat or transport the meat. There is no large town locally. Petropavlovsk is fifteen hundred kilometres away. For international trade there is no airport in the whole of northern Kamchatka, and no international seaport either. The Trans-Siberian Railway would have to be half as long again to reach us. Planes cannot land here, only helicopters, and to fly meat out the rate is extortionate.

'The state buys meat at twelve roubles per kilo. This is what they've been paying us. The selling-price now has a lot of tax added to it. If you add on transport costs as well, no Russian could afford to buy the meat. And all these prices are rising, except what we are paid for meat. The state promised to compensate us and has continued promising through three successive changes of government, but we've never seen a rouble of it. We have to believe they'll keep their word. What choice have we but to go on believing the lies?'

I asked tentatively about the Japanese market to the south.

'Export is easiest to Japan,' he admitted. 'The Japanese already buy as much fish as Kamchatka can sell, but they are not interested in meat. And anything handled via central government is liable to huge taxes at every turn. At this state farm the administration did succeed in selling a million roubles-worth of pantui to Japan, for pantocrin, but we have not been paid for it.'

Ruefully, he concluded, 'The state told us to go and find a

new market, but we have no contacts, no business experience, and no idea what to do. For the past seventy years we've had no free market, we have long forgotten how to conduct trade. It's difficult to become a commercial capitalist overnight. Next month there will be a special congress in Moscow to discuss these problems, but we can't go to it because we haven't got the money to pay the fares.'

Before I left I asked for his business card, he laughed and asked me by what name his country is called nowadays.

On the way back to Palana we flew into a blizzard and visibility was reduced to twenty metres, as we hugged the coast to find the way, flying below cliff height and just above the cracked icy sea.

Everyone except me was going home. Nadya was delighted, but insisted she'd enjoyed the whole trip. She recalled the title *Ten Days that Shook the World* and said her world would never be the same again. I had grown to admire Nadya's spirit. She was now eating normal Koryak meals and had conquered all the things that had terrified her when we set out. In the night I had dreamed she and I were standing with two camels beside a great snowy desert. I had suggested we ride the camels across the desert and she had said, 'I'm ready.' When I told her about the dream she responded, 'Yes, of course, I'd be ready.'

Nadya would be returning to the Itelmen village of Tigil. Everyone else lived in Palana, so I would see them again, since I planned to use Palana as a base for my travels over the next two weeks.

3
Palana

In Palana I stayed as a paying guest with Big Taya, a delightful huge fat Russian woman who didn't shake hands when she met me, she hugged me. She took me home, mothered me, and was my friend. Home was one of the identical apartments, each laid out inside exactly like its neighbour. Big Taya said this was supposed to be a sign of equality. The rooms were small. At lunch in the kitchen with four of us at a tiny table against the window there was hardly room to move. But the meal was delicious. Taya melted slices of pork fat to fry shallots and slabs of fresh reindeer meat, washed down with red bilberry juice and vodka. Her husband Vova was out fishing. She said he seldom caught anything but insisted on trying.

Varicose veins meant Taya was not an active person herself, but she grew vegetables outside the kitchen window in summer, and kept pots of chives in my room, which were often chopped and sprinkled on our soup with the explanation, 'Veetameen', since there are no fresh vegetables in Palana until summer, and that is barely long enough to grow vegetables successfully. Even the flour for bread is imported.

In Big Taya's apartment last year's vegetables and fruits, bottled in jars, were stacked high in every cupboard. With Taya's flair, most held wonderful concoctions like Maroshka, a sweet yellow northberry, tasting like guava, or Brusnika, a red bilberry, and ash-tree berries, tastiest after the first frost. Taya's favourite berry was Kniznika, like a purple raspberry, but hard to find. Another delicious one is Jumelis, honey-suckle berries, called the Kamchatka grape, and Taya described how their dark bloom seems to give the autumn meadows a blue haze. Everyone gathers berries in autumn, as many buckets and baskets as they can process and store against the lean months of winter.

When I first decided to come to Kamchatka I was told that by late winter there would be nothing to eat but putrid fish. It had been an offputting idea. And I had read, 'By the month of March all the store of fish is consumed, and the inhabitants begin to eat the fish usually given to dogs.' But Big Taya and her equally big husband seemed to spend much of their time eating. They had a meal at six p.m. when he came home, and another at nine p.m., and sometimes a midnight feast, too. While she talked, Taya fussed around pulling jars from the fridge and saying try this.

It was snowing hard. In the evening Big Taya suggested we went to the *banyo*, and asked me to choose from her range of scrubbing-toys to take with us: a rasp for making skin fresh, a long string of wooden rollers, birch twigs, and something that looked like stomach tripe. At the banyo, we were given a sheet, and went into a changing- and lounging-room. We stripped and made for a warm steamy room with stone slab floor and big metal pans for carrying water. I simply followed Big Taya's naked shape in the steam.

She stopped in a small steam room, its wooden terraced benches crowded with sweating flabby flesh. On their heads the women still wore assorted woollen hats. Several were in full facial make-up.

It was reassuring to meet the lithe shapes of Lisa, Taya and Inna from the dance group. Space was made for us and people tried to encourage me up to the top shelf. I named the shelves Nigeria, Cameroon, Congo and Gabon, and slowly made it to Gabon which was insufferably hot. I can't think why people enjoy it, except through masochism; they're all mad. After several turns between steaming and flogging each other with the birch twigs, showers, soapings, being hosed down with a high-pressure jet of cold water, cups of herbal tea, a honey face mask, and being rubbed with salt, I was feeling quite overcome and ended by having a massage for twenty roubles.

The masseur worked on the acupuncture system. He cured a lingering headache by pressing my elbow. And for the cough that caused it he used Red Star (like Tiger Balm) worked into various pressure points. He said the top vertebra should be rubbed if a person is feverish, between the eyebrows for sinus trouble, and to cure tiredness you should rub your nose with vodka for a minute so hard you cry with the pain.

Back home Taya gave me four stacks of photos to look through, showing their only child, a girl of twenty-one who married and moved away six months ago. I was intrigued by a photograph of the bride and groom biting a large loaf of bread without using their hands. A Russian custom, said Taya, then they light a fire on the ground beside a bowl of water, and jump through a hoop.

After the photos, Taya pounced on my phrase book with relish. 'Would you like a hot perm? A hair dye, blue rinse?' She offered me each. She had once been a hairdresser and beautician. I paused at the facial. Out came a pot of ginseng seeds mixed with oil, which she rubbed in wiggly lines down my face. It was very relaxing.

It was midnight before we retired to bed. A snowstorm raged all night. At seven a.m. I was woken by dogs and ravens squabbling over some bones. Ravens are useful as scavengers, but they kill other young birds and in autumn plunder geese nests for eggs and chicks. They are clever birds. People say that ravens are able to count, and of course if you are a Koryak you don't interfere with them.

I was watching the ravens through a tear in the net curtain. Taya pointed to the hole, and to the holes in the sleeves of her dress, laughing. Years ago it had had long sleeves, she said, but eventually the cuffs frayed, so she shortened the sleeves to her elbow. Now she would cut off the elbows to make it short-sleeved, and when that wore out, it would become sleeveless. It's not that things were expensive, they were simply not available. The cost of living was rising too, but at least rents were still reasonable. Taya's apartment cost fifteen roubles a month and houses in Palana only cost about five roubles more.

That day was a religious festival, although Palana had no church, and Taya said it would be a sin to speak ill of anyone today, or do menial chores like washing the floor, so having discovered in the banyo that Taya's neighbour Alexandra ran the Palana ski slope, I went skiing.

In the hut at the bottom of the slope I picked out some fairly short skis, knowing I was out of practice. The ski lift was a metal cable you clip a hook on, and balance on a toggle between your legs. Alexandra tutted at me for wobbling and letting go before we reached the top. She turned and raced past me saying, 'Follow me down.' She was an ex-Olympic skier and Master of Sport who had become slalom champion of the USSR in 1965. The Palana ski slope was entirely her baby, developed with small funding from local government. She now had a thriving school for a hundred to a hundred and fifty children. The piste was not wide, and it was studded with tree stumps and half-buried branches. I reached the bottom in undignified style and went up again, somehow holding on to the top. But I wished I hadn't because the top part of the slope was a steep mass of moguls, slush, branches and rocks. I fell frequently on the way down, jumping up and continuing quickly, hoping I hadn't said I knew how to ski. As the morning progressed I realised that if you can ski here, you can probably ski fearlessly anywhere. I arrived home cold and despondent, and Taya put a spoonful of her special honeysuckle jam in my tea for a treat.

In the afternoon I wen[t]
and his son. We wore hu[nting]
gear. To pull a sled is simpl[e]
my skis along, since the r[oute]
uphill was all right, down[hill]
threatened to overtake me an[d]
poles. Yuri didn't use poles, a[nd]
the shotgun.

We stopped to fish at a plac[e]
tween islands of alder trees. T[o]
snow from our skis before it froz[e]
later. Then we drilled a couple o[f]

Instead of the crisp crunching .... the dry ice at Old
Man's Creek, this was a wet sloppy sound. When we had no
luck with the fish, Yuri made a fire, tea was welcome, as was
the bread and caviar we laid out on a table of our upsidedown
skis. In Kamchatka you don't spread caviar thinly on toast,
you eat it with a large spoon. Though they all call it caviar, it
is in fact salmon roe, red and petit-pois sized. The quality is
not like the black caviar, but neither is the price. At the
moment it was only 250 roubles ($2.50) per litre. Elsewhere
in Russia it cost more, particularly in Ukraine and Belorussia
where it is considered effective against radiation.

A snowstorm began as we arrived back in Palana and it
continued through the night and the next day, but we went
out in it as I wanted to buy some thigh-length rubber waders
and Big Taya needed to do the shopping. Palana boasts
several shops, the state ones were as bare as those in the
north. We tackled food first, the emptiest shops of all, but
with queues of people the moment anything turns up to be
sold. We bought Gorby-Bush chicken, the result of a deal
with America, but more expensive than state meat.

Taya kept pulling out wads of *talon*, or food coupons, and
while we queued for bread she showed them to me. The
shopping allowance per person per month at state prices was:
tea 50 grams, rice 500 grams, sugar 1 kilo, butter 500 grams,

grams, chocolate half a bar, other sweets 200 grams, washing for three months, shampoo, a tube for were not a coupon item, so their cost half a rouble pre-perestroika to twenty-one ch. The coupon system has been in operation in atka for two and a half years, though some things like gar had been rationed before, if not as severely. The coupons allow you to buy at state prices: veal 60 roubles per kilo; pork 80 roubles; beef 50 roubles. When the coupons are finished one can buy at private shops more expensively. Kamchatka is giving away her gold and caviar in exchange for coupons, people said in the queue, outraged at rising prices. It was odd to see women I had last met naked in the banyo, now fully dressed. They all remembered me, I had more of a job to place them. Which steamy shelf had they sat on? My Russian speaking was improving but still elementary. Occasionally people shouted at me because they thought I couldn't hear.

My easiest response was to hand them my phrase book. But it wasn't a great help, being angled for businessmen and their wives visiting Moscow. In frustration of looking up words and not finding them and ploughing through sections called Airport to Hotel, The Hairdresser, Going to the Opera, I lost my patience and tore half the pages out of the book. 'No, don't throw them away,' Taya pleaded, and indeed everyone was keen to have the irrelevant pages for something to look at. As for Palana's own bookshop, I popped in there to look for postcards while Taya stayed in a queue; but there were no postcards in stock, and no modern novels, just old-fashioned textbooks and out-of-date moral literature.

We only got fresh fish because Big Taya's friend worked at the fish shop and had tucked some under the counter. The department store where we looked for waders had none, and its household range was three types of lampshade and two types of cloth for curtains. 'Do you see how we live?' exploded Taya. 'Why bother shopping? There's never anything to buy.'

We found a stack of waders in a private shop, and a pair cost me 125 roubles.

Afterwards we sat by the kitchen window drinking tea. An acquaintance of Taya's joined us for tea and when he left he mistook Taya's store cupboard for the front door, and walked into a cupboard crammed full of all the things she could not bear to throw away, plus spare winter clothing and jars of yet more berries. Everything began to fall off the shelves as the poor man backed out hastily and left blushing by the front door.

Taya said that rising prices and unemployment had led to an upsurge in burglary which had never existed under Communism. The banyo assistant's home had been burgled of everything, including his winter store of tins, but his neighbours would club together and give him what they could spare.

Big Taya had been retiling the bathroom. It was supposed to be a nice surprise, but all three of us were coughing from the grout fumes and it seemed as good a moment as any to move on to the fur-trading village of Lesnoe, 120 kilometres to the north, a post for the exchange of goods between coastal Koryak and reindeer Koryak. I shared a buran and sled with a trapper called Jena and his friend Yuri Z who was head teacher at Lesnoe School and said he could speak some English, though I found it very difficult to follow.

We set out in a blizzard and the journey deteriorated into a cross between a farce and a nightmare as we lost our way repeatedly in the white-out, broke through ice-bridges, wallowed into drifts and were nearly benighted. The snow-storm's vicious speed hurt in a way I had not known cold could. Even though I was wearing three layers of furs. It was perhaps just as well I didn't know about the death of three people travelling by buran like us between Palana and Lesnoe two months previously. They too had encountered a snow-storm and their bodies had not yet been found.

Darkness came when white went blue and light faded out of it. Jena stopped, located some wire and began improvising repairs to the headlamp. How would dark look in a white-out? At the next partly collapsed ice-bridge we didn't stop, just crossed our fingers and drove over the remaining metre-wide section, then made a slow haul up the opposite bank, wallowing in powder. When the engine overheated Jena packed snow on it. We were now short of fuel, since we were using a lot for this heavy work.

At last we struggled very late at night into Lesnoe. I stayed at Jena's and over the next few days met a lot of local trappers. The men from the coast barter their fish, walrus and whale blubber for reindeer hide, while in the strong-room of the Hunting Department I leafed through a Harrodsworth of mink and ermine, sable, red fox, wolverine and lynx. The smaller minkskins were turned inside out like tiny enve-lopes, both the ordinary mink and the yellow mink which in Kamchatka is almost white. In one shed I saw bearskins being cleaned and soaked in vats of water with bark shavings, then rescraped to make them supple. One hunter who has killed fifty bears in five years told me he received 106 roubles ($1) a skin. He is only allowed to sell them to the state. I asked how he could kill a bear for 106 roubles, it made no sense to me, but my question made no sense to him. Maybe I misunder-stood something in Yuri Z's very inadequate translation. Much more valuable is bear's bile which is used medicinally by the Japanese and Koreans for stomach complaints. The going rate I was told was 50 dollars a gram, and a bear has an average 50 grams of bile. How long, I wondered, before people exterminate bears for dollars.

Yuri Z was one of the town's ten per cent Russian minority. He vigorously despised all things Koryak, said the people were dirty, and disapproved of my interest in them. One day he dragooned me along to his school. In a large classroom his wife Ellen was thumping away at a piano and trilling a Russian song, while her class of five stared emptily into space. When I appeared she coerced three of them into singing, stretching their faces to reach the notes and frowning with concentration. In other classrooms children wearing mass produced clothes were looking blankly at books. There seemed no shortage of books and school materials, and the classrooms were airy, and decorated with local finds like Palaeolithic axes. The teachers were certainly trying to generate interest. I gave a short English lesson to the older classes and they asked a lot of questions about how people live in Britain. Yuri said the failure rate was appalling, as they were not interested in learning to be Russian. It was rare that anyone qualified for university.

Jena lent me some narrow cross-country skis and we went to visit a sacred site on a saddle between two hills. Bits of wool or ribbon tied to the branches of the trees showed how the Koryaks still venerated the spot. Jena made me close my eyes to take deep breaths, and before we left he said we must give something to the place. So we each took a matchstick, polished it and threw it toward the cliff behind us. 'This power is older than we are,' Jena said. 'If you bring a pendulum up here, it will swing in circles.'

In the afternoon I took a look around Lesnoe which is built on a low cliff above a river. The settlement was an uninteresting bunch of wooden buildings, small houses and some blocks of apartments, so I headed for the base of the cliff where several dog-teams were tethered. Each dog was chained just out of reach of the next, about ten to a group, with huts on stilts to store fish for dogfood. Here I met a Koryak man known to his friends as Lenin, and he agreed to take me next day to a place called Kinkil which was a village officially closed by the authorities. In theory no one lives there any more, all the Koryak inhabitants having been relocated by administrative order. Lenin was brewing a churn of dogfood which consisted of small putrid fish in ugly-smelling gravy. This fish gruel went with slabs of seal meat. It looked dreadful but the dogs were leaping with excitement.

Yuri turned up looking disapproving, but helped me finalise arrangements. That evening Jena, his wife Vera, and I went to dinner at Yuri's flat. Ellen had made an impressive effort with the food, and our plates were piled with things usually hoarded for special occasions, like tomatoes, peas and tinned pineapple. Vera hardly ate, just pushing her food around in a rude way. She obviously disliked Ellen too much to eat at her house. But when it came to the pudding she was caught by the gooey cake, with berries on top. We each had three helpings, Vera included. Then my side plate was filled with treacle, purpose unknown. The others ate it by the spoonful, so I put it in my coffee, where it seemed to go quite well. Yuri decided to give a slide show, and I insisted the subject be Kamchatka, knowing that would ensure it was not too long. We reached home at two a.m.

It was snowing hard when I awoke but, undaunted, Lenin turned up with his eight dogs whose harness was held together with many small bits of string. As usual everyone insisted on being sure I'd be warm enough, wrapping me in their clothes, scornful of my modern gear. I wanted the chance to use it, but people preferred me to do things their way.

We straddled the sled and left the village in chaos, the team having chased every other dog in sight, eight sets of jaws snarling and barking; it was the pack instinct that sent them hurtling towards all challengers, and we narrowly missed going both sides of a tree. The team got in a dreadful tangle but it couldn't be sorted out until we were clear of the village. When we stopped one dog leaped to attack the young black pup beside it, which ducked and lay submissive while the older one snarled. The pup was nine months old, learning the ropes. Lenin moved it beside an elderly splotched brown dog and we restarted. Lenin said his best dog was one of the leaders, Taiga, a sensible and shrewd-looking four-year-old, and his oldest was amiable Adam at nine years.

Training sled dogs starts at six months, putting them beside experienced dogs. The riff-raff of rattle-brained canines go in the middle, with the laziest near the sled. Lenin's team were a motley crew of laika and laika-trapper dog crosses. His driving was colourful with sounds, as he talked continually to the dogs in a series of clicks, raven squawks, ptarmigan cries, whistles, grunts, and words with staccato ends: *zit, omnitzah* (clever boy), *periot* (do it again). In between he talked about how to set the world to rights, and all the problems of hunters and trappers, which was why he was called Lenin, because he wanted to tell the world how to run its business.

We crossed a frozen river estuary and went along the coast within sight of the iced sea. This was still the Okhotsk Sea, which means hunters' sea. For travel on sea-ice Lenin pointed out that a dog-team was better than a buran, since the dogs could sense where the ice was dangerous. The flat beach stretched back into a flat plain with coastal hills and three peaks ahead of us. Lenin said a battle between Koryak and Itelmen had taken place on the tallest hill and the heads of the dead were stacked at the summit.

It was still snowing in large flakes, and the dogs' paws were getting compacted with ice. We paused to swop two more of them, putting a red Chow-like dog beside the pup. Lenin said he often switched their positions left and right to prevent them tiring in the muscles of one side only.

We met another dog-sled and both halted with only a metre to spare between the opposing lead dogs' noses. There seemed no clear rule about how to pass each other. Some of the dogs snarled and wanted to fight. The other man sat waiting for Lenin to manoeuvre round his pack. Lenin yelled at Taiga who moved left and with much whooping we slid past. If a dog-sled meets a reindeer-sled there's sometimes bloodshed; the dogs can tear the reindeer to bits, but Lenin said that fortunately it didn't happen here because the coastal plains are rich in fish to feed dog-teams. It is only far inland where there is no cheap fish that dogs are impractical and reindeer take over.

A little further on Lenin suggested I try driving, so we changed places. Most of the dogs seemed to be pulling well, though one devious sharp-nosed bitch slacked off whenever she thought I wasn't watching her. Other ropes were always taut and on downslopes they galloped along. Since I had been imitating Lenin's sounds for several kilometres, I now tried his run-faster noises. As the sled whooshed along we sometimes had to lean out to one side to counterbalance tipping. Suddenly the oldest dog, Adam, fell. The Chow behind jumped over him, Lenin grabbed the brake stick and we both flung our weight to the left as the sled veered and jerked the dogs to a standstill. To help the old dog, Lenin clipped its collar to a second string so it could trot without pulling. And he tied the pup's collar by a string to the main trace so it had to look ahead and could not try to turn around.

As we turned inland toward the coastal hills Lenin pointed to a thin patch of sea-ice and said a whale had broken through the ice there one year and come ashore to die, to the delight of the local fishermen. For some inexplicable reason whales regularly come ashore on Kamchatka's beaches. People have suggested perhaps they are affected by magnetic poles or secret radar activity, causing them to hit the coast. Or possibly submarines make ultra-sounds that disorient them.

'Giant fish, warrior, covered with chainmail, so big you look like a country, we cannot help you,' Lenin quoted from a local poet.

Coastal Koryak have an annual whale celebration which is based on the idea that its spirit will return to the ocean and bring a new whale the following year. If treated with hospitality the whale spirit may bring several of its living relatives, so it is symbolically given a bag of food for its journey, usually puddings.

Our backs were now to the snowstorm making it less unpleasant, but the ground became mushy and the dogs, though exuberantly willing, were floundering in drifts. We paused often to give them short breathers and let them cool down by rolling in the snow which they loved, scooping up mouthfuls of snow to cool their tongues.

Kinkil appeared in the distance, a few snowy roofs and old wooden store huts on stilts. We passed a small unkempt cemetery of wooden crosses. Lenin said they would be Even bodies because the Koryak cremate their dead. Before burning they stab the corpse to make sure it is dead, and cover the face with soot to stop the dead man seeing them. After the cremation they take a zigzag course home to lose the spirit, and are forbidden to look back. At the dead person's home they put hot embers from the fire outside his door, and fill the place with smoke to asphyxiate any lingering spirits and make sure the dead man's main soul doesn't try to come back. Along with a chief soul (*uyicit*), Koryaks have a second soul or 'breath' (*wuyici*) and a third soul, 'shadow' (*wuyil-wuyil*). The chief soul wanders the land for some time before going to the afterlife.

Lenin said several old people had died when Kinkil was closed and they had to move home. Two other local villages were closed down at the same time, though some people were now returning to one of them.

In Kinkil now there were just five wooden shacks. The shop had fallen down a year ago. At present the only inhabitants were an old man called Maxim and his wife.

We shared lunch, each contributing something; I'd brought some frozen deer meat from Talovka, Lenin provided tea and sugar, and Maxim had some smoked salmon. He said they live poorly in winter on seal meat and oil, and he also used the oil to waterproof his boots. River-fishing was impossible because the ice was three metres thick, far too much for a drill. His health had not been good ever since one hungry winter when he killed a bear and ate the meat. All bear meat

59

in Kamchatka is liable to a parasitic infection called trihinellos that, if the meat is untreated, can damage the human intestines and liver. If the eggs get into the bloodstream and hatch in your brain, you go mad. Death will come in the end. In Maxim the parasites had wormed all around his heart and lungs.

We reharnessed the dogs, and I drove again. Lenin said, 'Tell them some commands in English,' so I put in chirpy ones like 'Trot on,' 'At-a-boy,' and 'Gidd-i-up.' We kept up a good pace and had three decent gallops. The dogs grew hot and as soon as we slowed they all rolled heartily on their backs in the snow. To encourage them in the last stretch we played tricks like calling out, 'A hare, there goes a hare!' and they pulled again in excitement back to Lesnoe.

Next day I went out with Lenin again to visit a camp of reindeer-herdsmen. The way led through snow-layered forest, turning to spacious woodland known as light taiga. The driving was fast and problem-free, except when Max bit Ali. He attacks whichever dog is beside him. At this point a helicopter buzzed us and I could just make out someone waving enthusiastically at the porthole. It was Big Taya, pulled out of semi-retirement by the local administration and detailed to give haircuts to far-flung herders.

We found our camp in a birch clearing, and those young men who were not stupifyingly drunk came out to say hello. It was a depressing scene. They talked wildly about hating the Russians, and while they ranted I saw the empty bottles were not vodka, but cologne, which is often drunk here when vodka is not available. In this disorderly camp there was no fresh food and we were offered some distinctly putrid fish. When we left they gave me a hunting knife with a handle of deer horn, and I gave them a mouth organ. One lad played it, while another demonstrated that the knife was sharp by unfortunately cutting his own finger, which everyone helped him to bandage.

Lenin and I headed on among some open hills. He was

driving. As we slid over the crest of a hill the dogs saw three reindeer just a hundred metres from our path and began baying and straining at their harness. Lenin kept them under control until suddenly one of the bits of string on a harness snapped, and the bad-tempered Max was free. He shot away in pursuit of the deer who began floundering in drifts, while Max flew on top of the crust. Lenin and I hauled on the brake to try and hold the remaining seven dogs, and things started happening fast. While I leaned all my weight on the brake, Lenin set off after Max who by now had leapt on the deer's back. It fell, got up, shook off the dog and ran again. My seven dogs were howling, yelping and straining at the sled. I clung on.

The deer under attack was young, none too strong, and no match for the old dog's hunting instinct. At his next jump they both fell in the snow, and Max ripped its throat out. This was all too much for the leading dogs who swung sideways in the harness, jerking at the sled. I was still glued to the brake pole but this was designed to stop the sled going forwards, and the sideways jolt pulled both me and the brake from the ground as the whole pack joined the hunt. With the useless brake in one hand, I hung on to the sled with the other as it dragged me along, faster and faster, snow pouring into my clothing, dogs baying. On a hard stretch of crust my arm gave way and I let go.

Without stopping to dust the snow from my face, I began to run after the dogs as hard as I could in my encumbering clothes, still clutching the brake. Lenin was also chasing after the sled and yelling at Taiga to stop, and at last she slowed. They were all milling around in their tangled harnesses as I reached the sled and jumped on to it, jabbing the brake in again, and gasping for breath. Lenin arrived. There was no sign of Max and the deer. We drove quickly back over the hill crest, and saw Max still tearing at his prize. This time Lenin managed to catch Max and I just managed to make a better fist of holding the other seven.

Returning to Lesnoe some hours later, Lenin let me drive

again. In front of me on the sled was the reindeer's stomach and long intestine, and at every jolt the intestine slithered and slopped around in a slimy way. When loops slid off and trailed in the snow I had to grab them quickly before the runners went over them. With every nick in the skin, the contents oozed on to my legs. It's only processed vegetable I told myself. Fortunately Lenin had not had to pay for the dead deer, and the herders had given him the stomach as a present. They would use the carcass for their meat supply. I think Lenin had ticked them off soundly, and had told them they were doing a lousy job as herdsmen. The deer, a yearling, should have weighed thirty kilos but it was a thin twenty kilos, undernourished because the herdsmen couldn't be bothered to move the herd to fresh pasture. Back in Lesnoe we cut up the intestine into the dog meal.

Lenin said we would need two extra dogs for our journey back to Palana and would borrow them from the postman, Mr Billows Nakent, so we went to call on him. Every month he did an eight-hundred-kilometre mail round by dog sled and said that in good weather he could get across the neck of the peninsula in two days. Now sixty-five, he had been postmaster here all his life. He also ran the local telephone exchange, with his wife as stand-in. His daughter sold stamps in a kiosk, but she was too shy to tell me the cost of one. I wrote some postcards home and wondered how soon they would arrive.

By now I had developed a cough and cold, from one or other of my soakings, so Lenin insisted I drink something he called Golden Root. He took me to his home and prepared the root by scraping it, then chopping it up and infusing it as tea. The root felt squidgey, but Lenin swore it cured all ills and made me drink several cups. By the fourth I was beginning to feel very merry. By the fifth I was demonstrating the four movements of the Hololo dance, complete with drum accompaniment. All Lenin's five daughters joined in. I awoke next morning with a cracking headache and a worse cough.

*

The freeze in the night was not enough to harden the snow so, as it was too slushy for a long dog-sled ride, I cast around for alternative transport back to Palana.

A *vezdehod* had arrived the previous night, and I watched it unloading some glass windows and building materials for a new shop. A vezdehod is an all-terrain tank-style vehicle with caterpillar tracks that can cope with almost anything. The driver said he would be going back to Palana later that day and had enough space for me. So I decided on a relaxing morning which was the only thing I was capable of. My head clanged when I moved, my brain felt squeezed by tight metal bolts. Vera said she thought the Golden Root tea stimulated one's blood pressure and I'd had an overdose. It felt like a monstrous hangover.

The vezdehod's cargo had included the newspapers for Lesnoe. Vera said they were already a week old, which I thought was not bad for such an out-of-the-way place, but she thought it poor.

Eventually my baggage was flung in the back and I scrambled high up in the front where it was wide enough for five or six adults to sit abreast with a great view out of the windscreen panels at a leaden sky. The machine clanked deafeningly, its gauges dead but for an occasional flicker into agitated action. Then we set off crossing rivers and streams, stretching forward on to ice-bridges, where I felt sure we would nosedive in. I couldn't understand how the snow held our weight. I doubted there was much left of the bridges. In woodland the vezdehod was like a battering ram, simply crushing whatever was in its path. I couldn't even hear the small trees breaking, except the ones that hit the windscreen. We had a tight squeeze in one place to pass between two sturdy trunks. The driver had gashed them both last time, but this was the only Palana to Lesnoe track. Vezdehods were certainly bad news for woodland conservation. However, to build proper roads in Kamchatka is impractical because of earthquakes and permafrost. In summer the top few metres of permafrost thaw into slush, and the foundations of roads and bridges sink and collapse. Bridges can be achieved using hollow concrete pillars, or kerosene-filled metal supports which do not thaw, but there are additional problems as springtime river levels rise with melting snow and great chunks of ice can easily sweep away bridges.

With a crack a metal plate on the caterpillar track broke and we stopped for repairs, twenty people pouring out of the vezdehod's central section for a breath of fresh air. I took a look at the tracks, each over a metre wide, made of two-centimetre-thick rubber with metal ridges bolted on. Three had cracked and needed more bolts to hold them in place. Each track had six wheels, plus two big cog sections. The vehicle didn't have scratches from fighting trees and rocks, it had great dents and scars.

We came to a broken ice-bridge and just drove over the metre gap with no trouble. We 'jumped' two more streams then drove up into some hills, avoiding the route along the river-ice, my angle of vision changing steeply up and downhill as we flipped over the ridges.

Big Taya was waiting for me at the Palana bus stop at ten p.m., pulling a small sled for my luggage. She hugged me and we went home to one of her special Gorby-Bush chicken suppers. Sadly, Vova her husband was in and out of hospital with a bad cough (I think from the retiling fumes). I was still coughing a lot, too, and holding my head from the tea, so Taya pulled out all her jars of medicine: vodka and cedar-bush nuts, bits of roots, and bear's bile; fungus, ginseng seeds, and chopped dried herbal remedies. Some jars had labels, but not all. She said Lenin had given me 'Rhodiola Rosea' and we could overcome its effects with a tisane of daisy flowers, wild rose-hips and powdered leaves of blackcurrant. She also rubbed me with ginseng oil. But I didn't sleep that well.

The Beringei dog-sled race was due to pass through Palana

next day. It was only the second year it had been run and was billing itself as the longest race in the world, being 1,980 kilometres against the Iditarod's 1,738 kilometres in Alaska. Ten dog-teams had set out a week ago from a place in the interior with the unlikely name of Esso and they would take three more weeks to reach the finishing-line at Marco.

In view of my recent dog-sled-driving experience with Lenin, Vova suggested we take a buran down to the Palana river to watch and we were joined by the geologist called Valodya whose company had provided the invitation that allowed me to come to Kamchatka. He said the invitation had cost someone a television set. I was indeed fortunate to have received a permit.

Two dog-teams came into view close together, thirteen dogs to a team, the men darkly tanned and rimed in frost, urging their dogs on. We shouted encouragement and waited for more to happen, but it turned into a bit of a non-event, not helped by the buran keeping breaking down. The fanbelt had snapped. We improvised repairs but oily smoke poured out every time Vova tried to start the engine and the cord he used for pull-starting was fraying strand by strand. By the third pull it was broken halfway across. Eventually Valodya and I started walking the ten kilometres home, leaving Vova saying, 'It'll start in a moment.'

Valodya told me about Palana's various sacred stones which have had offerings made to them from Palaeolithic times. One looks like a pregnant woman and if a man can lift it, he will live a long life. Others have a reputation for moving mysteriously about for their own reasons and disapproving of being moved by man for theirs. A stone at Tilichiki so objected to being incorporated into a monument that the truck drivers who shifted it were killed soon after in an accident and the family who were keepers of the monument lost their eldest son at sea.

Valodya went on to talk in a melancholy Russian way of the immensity and solitude of the tundra. 'Day follows day with no colours and you begin to think you could disappear for ever in this boundless space, forgotten in the universe. It's important not to think of yourself as a transient being. You have to believe you will go on for ever. Otherwise you will be overwhelmed.'

Our heads were white with hoarfrost, not unusually; I was getting used to having eyelashes matted with ice. We walked into Palana in the dusk through the dog-sled-race finishing-line. A small crowd still waiting for more arrivals had lit a bonfire to keep warm. The main problem, said one musher, was that the route was hardly marked, and after midnight, when the majority came in, they were in a rage because they had got lost. The last sled came in at six a.m. The next day was a rest day, but they all got so drunk on vodka in the evening that only one competitor turned up the following morning at the starting-line. So the race was adjourned for an extra day.

It was the birthday of Tanya, a dentist neighbour, and she invited Big Taya and me to a lunch party. Big Taya struggled into a black velvet dress with sequins and some rarely available tights. She said she heard Western women can afford to wear tights once then throw them away. I said nonsense.

For a gift we were meant to bring a flower, but Taya had none so we took a sprig of chives. Taya also gave Tanya four sideplates, and I gave her a small bar of soap and a lipstick, someone gave her some material for sewing, someone else a fish slice. The guests were interestingly varied in their origins: Vavic was a Kamchadal, Sasha from Belorussia, Taya was Russian, and Luda came from the Ukraine, her husband having been expelled from there eight years ago. Those who were able to keep on their homes further west would have three-month annual holidays in which to return to them, and high salaries for the hardship of working in such a remote spot.

Russia has always encouraged migration east, even Gorbachev promoted the Far East as a land opportunity, and back in the nineteenth century when Russia colonised Alaska such migrants were essential. By 1817 there were six hundred Russians in Alaska. The first maps of America's north-west were made by Russians, and the first gold deposits there were located by these colonisers.

The table was spread with a large joint of pork, bowls of caviar, fish, cheese, mushrooms, stuffed eggs, pork fat, grated carrot, pickled cabbage. For the toasts we had Bulgarian whisky and Russian vodka. Everyone else finished the glass at a gulp of course. After the third I could only sip.

As the main topic of conversation they all complained about life in Russia, rising prices and deficits. My own problem was turning out to revolve round a conspicuous lack of variety in Russian names. Everybody seemed to choose one from the ten commonest. Vladimir is shortened to Valodya, or Vova or Vovik, and Yuri said there were four Yuris in his class at school. I had already met three so could believe it. Looking round the table, I noticed that Russians wear a wedding ring on their right hand if married, on left hand if divorced. I wear what we call a Russian ring, made up of three separate bands that can come apart but stay interlinked, but the Russians said they had never heard of such a thing themselves. The conversation veered from marriage to virgins. Sasha said that Kamchatka had been instructed by Catherine the Great to send six virgins to her Imperial court. The virgins were selected and dispatched on their long journey, so long indeed that before they were halfway there every one of them was pregnant, and by the time the Kamchatka virgins reached the Imperial court, they each had a couple of children.

At eight the next morning I went with Taya to the main square to watch the Beringei Race set off again. There were only five teams left now. One musher was putting homemade leather paw-guards on some of his dogs to protect them. The excitement had gone out of the affair because it was clear who would win, a Russian from Chukotka, called

Radivelov who was leading so far, and so he should, as he had more experience, training and dedication than the rest put together. Each sled-team went to the starting-line in turn, a countdown from ten to zero and away they rushed. Number Two sled took off at speed and went the wrong way. Some bystanders hurried to help stop the sled and turn the dogs.

Victor, a tall young Russian who was besotted with race dogs, said the Beringei did not count since it had no experienced race dogs. Real racers do 150–200 kilometres per day and keep it up for 1,800 kilometres. The ones we were watching could only manage 50–70 kilometres a day. Though the international race champions in Alaska and Canada now take the lead with all the most recent technical aids, the tradition of sled-dog-racing originated centuries ago in Siberia and Chukotka, and he went on to regale me with cunning wheezes designed to upset a competitor, like dropping pieces of dried fish on the ground to distract those coming behind, or rubbing bear's grease on a rival's sled, which makes his dogs keep turning around.

As the final team were being harnessed one of the dogs escaped, vanishing down a side alley in pursuit of a town dog. It took an hour of chasing around before it was captured, reharnessed, and the sled rejoined the race.

Victor said he had twenty-four dogs and ten puppies in training, and offered to show them to me later that day. Over a lunch of fried salmon, smoked salmon, salmon caviar, and salad, he told us how he first came to Palana in 1987, skiing from Ossora which took twenty days. A trapper friend met him forty kilometres from town with a dog-sled, and Victor was hooked. He decided he needed his own sled, and tried to settle in Palana, but he had continual trouble with the authorities. Someone set a police watch on him. So one night he packed his sled, made ready the dogs, and vanished into the tundra. For three months the police could not find him, and he got to know northern Kamchatka the hard way, but when he returned to Palana, he had no more trouble from the police. Perhaps he had served his apprenticeship.

As we walked to visit his dogs, Victor told a romantic story of a musher friend who eloped with the Inuit girl he was 'given' as a birthday present, and married her, despite the girl's father giving chase in a vezdehod. Victor was a witness at the wedding.

Victor had never managed to raise the sponsorship to race his own team in the Yukon Quest Fairbanks to Whitehorse dog race, so he had become a handler for the famous Doug Bowers team, which is where he had learned his English. We reached the village where his dogs lived, and admired the ten young pups, all from one litter, not yet a year old. Two dogs were large with white bandit markings on eyes and forehead, four more were smaller, which Victor preferred because they have more energy. Big dogs grow tired quickly and need more food. Four were bitches, which he said are more intelligent and two of these were destined to become lead dogs. 'My best girl is Mucha. It means mosquito. She can sprint a short distance at thirty kilometres per hour.'

He was also looking after two dogs that dropped out of the Beringei Race. One had eaten a lemming and within twenty-five kilometres had become paralysed in the back legs. The other was a Koryak dog whose heart was not good enough to continue racing, according to the vet, though he could still be a working dog. Tethered near him was a handsome red Chow-like dog which Victor explained came from Chukotka and had been left on loan for breeding to bring some new blood to the local trapper bitches.

He showed me his sled, built to a racing design, not a Koryak one. It was three and a half metres long and weighed sixteen kilos. You sit on or straddle Koryak and Chukchi sleds, but you stand at the back of these racing sleds, on the end of the runners, and the brake is a semi-circular metal piece with two long metal teeth which you stamp down on. Koryak and Chukchi sleds are made for work. Sport is a new idea. Victor had been bemused by finding that in Alaska there was no concept of working dogs, only dogs for sport.

Another difference is in the diet: race dogs do not eat fish, they are fed deer meat and crushed wheat, plus whale meat. Victor had some spongy yellow blubber and fibrous red flesh from a whale that recently came ashore. Like Lenin, Victor knew about the whales in the Okhotsk Sea and once became so absorbed in watching them while sledding along on the sea-ice that he was caught by the incoming tide, hemmed in by cliffs three metres tall. The tide rose, flooding the ice. The dogs paddled on, the water grew steadily deeper, there was no way up the cliff. Finally, in desperation, Victor unharnessed his dogs and managed to throw them one by one up on to the clifftop, before climbing up himself and hauling his 250-kilo laden sled after him.

Across the food store from the whale blubber was a pile of frozen deer innards, and a shape I went to investigate.

'What's the dead dog for?'

'It's frozen. I'm keeping it until hunting season, then I'll use it as bait. If you put out dead dog, it's like making a restaurant for foxes.'

In another shed two men were working at making snow-shoes, looping walrus thong on a light birch frame to give tension to the web holding one's boot. There are different types of snowshoe depending on a person's height, the type of snow, or terrain. Mountain snowshoes have two metal prongs to prevent backsliding on ice. The word for snowshoe in Russian is *sneg-o-stoep* which literally means snow step. In Koryak they are called *Lapka*, which means web-foot, as in ducks and cormorants.

A new sled runner was being set in the correct front arc. The wood had to be made supple enough for such a tight bend by heating it in a metal tube filled with water, and after it had steamed for some hours it was slotted into a wood mould to set as it dried.

We went back for tea at Victor's apartment, very much a

bachelor pad with boots on the radiators, ten pairs of socks drying in the bathroom, and dog harnesses looped tidily over hooks. He gave me his photo album to look at while he made tea. It showed a string of girlfriends. Taya said all the girls went for Victor because he was young, wealthy and enterprising; indeed he was thirty-four, divorced and good-looking, though it was odd when he smiled to see his complete row of shiny steel teeth. Victor's father kept bees in the Altai-Ural Mountains and we put spoonfuls of his honey in our tea.

The thaw was continuing, though could refreeze any day. Masses of snow fell but with the temperature at only −5° it was not enough to make it firm. It felt almost like spring. One day Big Taya said, 'Today is a holiday called Provodizimai which means goodbye to the worst of winter. In the town square we'll burn an effigy of a woman.' Winter (*zimmer* in Russian) has female gender.

We went to the main square, still dominated by a statue of Lenin, where crowds of people surrounded a makeshift stage in front of the ex-Communist Party Headquarters, now the Koryak National Association administration. Various local artistes performed music and dance, and the Russians sang songs of their home towns.

The effigy, in her skirts, bonnet and grass hair, burned easily, despite the falling snow, and we warmed our hands at her fire.

Later Taya and I went to visit Vova who had not shaken off his chest cough and was back in hospital. Taya took food to him every day. In fact she fed all six patients in his ward. The corridors were plastered with posters of heroic nurses in action in the string of wars Russia was obliged to have to train its oversized army. The patients kept saying how awful it all was, and I said not at all, it was just the same as any National Health hospital, except that this one had probably run out of medicines.

In the evening Taya said she would trim my hair, which I agreed to, though still refusing the perm she kept offering from the torn-out pages of my guide book. Old hairdressers never give up. With scissors in hand she turned into a demon, chopping and snipping – 'Please, just a trim.' 'Yes, yes, I'm not doing anything' – as she whipped out a load of curlers and a bottle of liquid, and rolled my hair up on wooden rollers held by thin strips of old bicycle inner tube. What on earth would I look like in the morning? I tried to explain to Taya that, as a traveller, it is not wise for me to try to be pretty, since men might think it was to attract them. The plainer the better. Her response was if that stuff I put on your hair goes wrong, we may have to shave your head.

Having not satisfied her creativity on me she began squeezing tubes of colour dye on to a plate. Blue dye. I asked, 'For you or me?' Her. Fine, she had brown hair which could be good with a touch of dark blue. I told her she was a punk, and asked what Vova would say.

'Nothing, in the past I've dyed it red, yellow, every colour!' Blue dye flew as she vigorously rubbed her hair. In the morning I had a riot of curls, Taya's hair was black, and there were blue fingerprints all through my dictionary.

For breakfast Taya put out all the things I'd not yet eaten and said I must finish them up: one cold fish, some venison stuffed in cabbage leaves and a slab of cake. She was busy making sweets of uncooked cake mix, to be eaten raw.

The airport runway had been unusable for a week; it re-opened on the day my ticket was scheduled. When I packed to leave Palana, Taya kept bursting into tears. She had been a good friend to me and I loved her warm heart. Before leaving the house we observed the Russian tradition that requires everyone to sit in silence for a minute. It means one day you will come back.

At the airport my ticket to Petropavlovsk confused the clerk who had not seen a foreign-style air ticket before and said 'Where is the coupon? I have to tear out the coupon.' It became so complicated they insisted on selling me a ticket with coupon at local prices, twenty-four dollars for the flight, whereas my foreign one had cost three times the price. Big Taya was with me, she wouldn't leave until I boarded the plane, and tears poured down her face again as she hugged me in farewell.

4

Petropavlovsk

'Hold on, here comes an earthquake.'

I was having lunch in the Terminus Restaurant at the harbour in Petropavlovsk. As the tremor passed a few glasses rattled but it was only about three on the Richter Scale, and within a minute it had gone. A week before there had been a quake which reached six, its epicentre a hundred kilometres out to sea. None had caused as much damage as the 1971 quake which measured ten, but of course we had heard nothing about its aftermath in the West because of the Soviet Union's obsessive secrecy about any demoralising news, even events for which they could not be blamed.

We went back to our fern salad and king crab. My companions were Valodya whose company was based in Petropavlovsk and Natasha, a twenty-four-year-old interpreter whom I was hoping to take with me on my next leg of travels. Valodya said that in the twenty-six years that Kamchatka and the Komandor Isles have been seismically recorded there had been forty thousand notable quakes. In fact there are minor earthquakes almost every day.

'How you feel an earthquake,' he explained, 'depends on whether your hut or house is built on rock, giving a hard friction quake, or swamp which usually produces a more gentle rocking motion. Normally the first wave is vertical, the second is horizontal.' To make buildings quake-proof they are built in sections, attached to great wooden piles that go deep into the ground.

After lunch we walked round the harbour, its docks stacked with timber and barrels of fish. Most of the immense catch was destined for Japan. There was once a great plan to build a sea salt extraction plant to salt the fish for export farther afield. But it proved to be one of those misconceived schemes that failed to take into account the high iodine content of Kamchatka salt. Avacha Bay is a lovely natural harbour, bordered by the hilly range of Petropavlovsk's spacious residential suburbs, ending in a rugged cliff, and the long graceful curve of the far side of the bay with yet more snowy volcanoes behind it to the south. Floating plates of ice, well cracked and broken by the comings and goings of cargo boats, filled the bay. I watched a submarine cruising on the surface. The nuclear submarine factory here was a contributing reason why Kamchatka used to be closed to outsiders. Not even other Soviet citizens were allowed to come to Kamchatka without a permit.

Valodya wanted to show me a monument which stands outside the old Communist Party Headquarters. He said the building had been locked for a week when the Communist Party was ousted, then it opened again as the new regional government office and all the same people came back wearing different hats and spouting different ideology. The building had an impressive pillared facade, and in front of it, half buried in snow, was an obelisk.

'This small piece of land belongs to Britain,' Natasha said helping me to scrape back the snow so we could read the inscription.

The words became visible: 'Sacred to the memory of Captain Charles Clerk RN who died August 22, 1779, whose body is interred beneath this stone. This monument was erected by the Lords Commissioner of the Admiralty of Great Britain to mark their appreciation of the brave and honourable career of a gallant British officer.'

Clerk had been second-in-command to Captain Cook. He had been on Cook's two previous voyages, finding the Australian Barrier Reef, determining New Zealand's position and trying to find Antarctica. For the third round-the-world expedition, Britain sent two ships, *Resolution* and *Discovery*. Cook was captain of *Resolution*; the Commander of *Discovery* was the thirty-three-year-old Clerk. In 1776 the expedition set out with tasks which included navigating into the Bering Strait from the Pacific and discovering one end of the mysterious North-West Passage to the Atlantic.

On their way north Cook was killed in Hawaii and Clerk became expedition leader. He reached Petropavlovsk in 1779 and was treated with hospitality. He sailed on north until, seriously ill with consumption, he was forced back to Petropavlovsk where he died, aged thirty-eight. In 1913 a delegation from the British Admiralty visited the town and settled this monument over his grave.

Peter I had sent two expeditions to Kamchatka looking for the North-West Passage at the end of the seventeenth century. The actual confirmation that the passage to the Atlantic existed was a two-bite affair, since Bering who found the strait didn't try to see what lay beyond. The Russian Admiralty sent him back again to do the job properly.

Natasha showed me some notes she had translated about the Bering expedition. A month before Bering died in 1741 he wrote 'In a grim stormy night the shrouds of *St Peter* [his ship] were torn; no longer was it possible to carry sails ... and it was decided to head for the land and anchor near it. The rotted anchor rope broke, and the ship was swept by the surf towards the rock-fringed shore. The second anchor was also wrenched off. Luckily a bigger wave heaved us over the rocks and delivered us into quiet waters.' It was Avacha Bay. Bering founded Petropavlovsk, naming it after his two ships, *St Peter* and *St Paul*.

I stayed in a hotel on the outskirts where the city backs up to a group of three volcanoes. From my window I watched the central one, Avacha, belching steam. Once it was the largest of the group but it blew its top off a long time ago. The largest now is Koryaksky at nearly four thousand metres, but Avacha is still the most active, last erupting in 1990 when the whole city watched awestruck as red-hot flows of lava poured into the night.

That evening, as I was ploughing through my dish of herring and red cabbage, Valodya said, 'Don't turn round now but you'll notice there's two tables of mafia in here.' These were Koreans and Chechnyas from a republic near Georgia: the Koreans I recognised while the Chechnyas were swarthy and black haired.

'What do the mafia do?' I asked.

'They moved in as soon as Kamchatka opened, filling all the niches not taken by the state, and working rackets with private companies trying to start up. The mafia imports a lot of vodka to trade with Koryaks. And they're heavily into gold. They don't pay for it, they demand it from mining enterprises as protection money.'

The place was empty but for us and them. The hotel restaurant was reputed to be one of the best in town, although it always had stale bread, no sugar for the coffee, and sometimes no coffee or tea either. Most other bistros only gave you spoons to eat with because Kamchatka had a critical shortage of forks.

The following evening I was taken out to dinner at the mafia's own restaurant, in a class by itself. Dishes loaded with delicacies were spread all over the table and as soon as you ate one, another appeared. Each table in its discreet dining booth had its own dinky waitress, hovering to be called. The atmosphere was intriguing, as if countless Korean ears were listening to what we said. Again we were the only other diners.

Earlier a thief had broken into the car I had hired for the day and stolen a torch and screwdriver. They said he was a mafia man looking for my camera because I had taken pictures at the black-market bazaar for hardware, car parts, metal tools, and bric-à-brac. It had made some people very nervous. Apart from that, my tour of the city had been enjoyable. Petropavlovsk, along with the nearby airport town of Elizovo, accounts for over half the population of Kamchatka. That is 250,000 out of a total population of 450,000. While I was there I saw a religious rally held by Bahai missionaries who had recently arrived. The missionaries were American, Natasha told me, and she didn't like them.

'We Russians may be godless, but they act like we're still savages.'

At the regional headquarters I met a diminutive moon-faced lady who discussed the Koryak National Association with me and suggested I should travel with a gun. Why? I wondered aloud.

'To shoot troublesome people,' she replied blandly.

'What would your government say if I said sorry I just shot some people?' I asked, rather shocked.

'Well, against bears, then,' she conceded.

That sounded more reasonable but I hoped unnecessary. It reminded me of the Russians in Moscow who say Kamchatka is where people equal bears in numbers and looks, and both live in caves.

In mid-April I moved south from Petropavlovsk for a couple of days in a volcano region, staying in a cabin warmed by permanent heating from pipes drilled into underground hot sources. The hut belonged to a vulcanologist called Boris from the Institute of Vulcanology in Petropavlovsk who used it as a base for testing the water temperature and mineral content of the numerous hot springs, and he agreed to show me round. I put on my new wading boots, and we strode off into the deep snow, toiling uphill to a group of five hot springs where Boris took mineral samples. He makes earthquake forecasts on a regular basis, and said that two days before an earthquake the underground cracks open emitting light gas and Radon which is naturally radio-active. Twenty-nine of Kamchatka's 180 volcanoes are among the most active in the world. Vulcanologists worldwide visit the region and nowhere else except Hawaii has such a variety of lava, geysers, and different types of volcanic activity. The volcanoes and earthquakes, Boris explained, are separate and independent results of the movement of tectonic plates, three of which meet and grind beneath Kamchatka which is also part of the 'ring of fire' that circles the Pacific. Klyuchevskaya is the area where the Pacific, Eurasian and North American plates meet and most of its twelve volcanic cones are tall enough to dwarf Vesuvius or Etna. Three are over 4,000 metres. Klyuchevskoy (4,750 metres) has erupted sixty times in 200 years. The last time, in 1983, it threw up 200 million cubic metres of magma, the glaciers began to melt, and eighty million tons of hot water poured down into the valleys.

Even more impressive was the story of Ksudach's eruption way back in March 1907, which blasted out one square kilometre of rock. The land went dark and for a thousand kilometres in every direction the black sky rained sand and ash. As far away as Europe the daylight was darkened, and sunrises and sunsets were coloured strange deep reds.

The first spring we reached was warm not hot, and had green mosses and algae growing in it, the first non-dormant plants I'd seen in Kamchatka.

I asked Boris which volcanoes would be next to erupt and he reeled off a whole list of likely candidates. Most volcanoes in Kamchatka are young and boisterous. The newest is Chucheska Hill, created only seven thousand years ago.

We tacked along the contour of the hill and had a long slide down to the second spring. Warm streams often undermine the snow, either hidden beneath it, or open with snowbridges. Boris called the stream tunnels the 'Kamchatka Underground Line.' Once he fell into a tunnel too deep to climb out from, and followed it for an hour before he found a hole he could use for an exit. Striding back downhill in thigh-deep snow, I pulled my waders to full height and felt invincible.

After lunch of bread and caviar we put on cross-country skis and Boris offered to show me where the salmon come to spawn. At the end of the creek a poacher had strung his net. It was a bit early to catch anything, Boris said, but when the fish do arrive, some of the river mouths get traffic jams of salmon. During this time the adult fishes' noses grow a beak with large teeth. They all turn bright red, their spawning colour, stop feeding and start to die. The fishermen only take the caviar, as the flesh does not taste good, and they throw the carcasses back to provide food for the hatching spawn, who consume the microbes that feed on the rotting fish. This excellent fertiliser also ensures giant meadowsweet and cow parsley on the banks downstream of the spawning grounds.

I struggled to keep pace on my skis as Boris forged along beside the stream, its banks of snow overhanging the water. Waiting for me to catch up, Boris stood quoting poetry, which he often did, then said, 'We can tell when the fish are starting to come upriver because the bird called the Chichivitsa calls "Chui-chui, chui-chui", and the dog rose begins to bloom. If the dog rose is late the fish will also be late. That's because if spring is too wet for the dog rose, the river levels will be high, the fish will be waiting at sea for the right conditions and shallow spawning grounds.'

I was surprised to see a river that was not frozen, and Boris showed me how to cross it, side-stepping down the bank, skis and all, in our rubber wellies. Where the river had changed its course in the last year we had to find ways across several narrow gulleys, either by lunging sideways or looking for snow-bridges to ski over. Boris said the rivers often did this, confounding his maps.

When the weather became foul, pelting wet snow in a fierce wind, we returned to the hut and Natasha and I went for a banyo at a hot spring with a shed built over it. Instead of a

80

cold tap there was a shovel stuck in the snow. With supper Boris provided a liqueur made from vodka plus syrup of dog rose, nettle, pears, and ash-tree fruit, and told stories about walking to work here which took several days before the road was made. This, he confessed, was probably because they used to carry moonshine vodka for the journey and would fall into holes and swamps. 'Ah, if you have never been silly,' said Boris 'it means you have never been young.'

It was skis and wellies again next day, and heavy going because I was not used to the narrow touring skis and the snow was so soft they sank in. The first major downhill I swooshed down and only fell at the bottom; the next was more exhilarating until my ski got trapped under a branch and I fell flat on my face in the snow. But it was all good prac-tice for travel in the wild volcanic region I wanted to visit next, where I would need to be proficient. As the day wore on, the wind blew harder, making the branches of the trees rattle and dump loads of snow at unexpected moments.

None of the rivers and tributaries here were frozen and in the afternoon we reached a stream without any snow on its boulder-strewn banks, as a thermal base made the rocks warm. We stopped here for a picnic lunch, and, because the minerals of this water are bad for teeth, quenched our thirst with handfuls of snow.

On the way back we saw tracks of Arctic hares, and Boris said one year there was so much volcanic ash that instead of turning white the hares had gone grey. He lapsed again into poetry and an occasional Russian song. Natasha said she had seen the phenomenon of red snow, which appears on glaciers in summer, when the air is a warm 20° and snow lies in shaded places, making conditions right for bacteria. This red or pink bacteria grows on the snow's surface. Further north, she said, it looked red, but in Kamchatka it tended to make the snow pink.

The next morning we felt fit enough to go climbing. It was only blowing what Boris described as a middle blizzard when

81

we set out up a mountain called Gariachi. Above our ravine the wind was tearing along. Occasionally we glimpsed the sun as a pale orb in the blizzard. The snow deepened and we progressed by crawling along on hands and knees, spreading our weight. My hands often fell through to the shoulder, my knees worked better, though I would have had no marks for style. Half-blinded by the blizzard, up we toiled until the snow was again hard enough to allow wading on foot.

The ravine grew steeper, Boris began mumbling about avalanches but I didn't take him seriously. Natasha developed a nosebleed that we wiped up with snow. As we went higher the temperature dropped, the blizzard intensified, but now the saddle between the peaks was not far. We took it in turns to lead, up the centre of the couloir, the hardest and best snow. Boris's warnings of avalanche grew more persistent, but it was not until Natasha translated, 'Now we're playing with death if we try to go further,' that I understood the danger. The top really wasn't far.

'Do you want to go back down?'

'Do you?'

'We'll just go to the saddle.'

Natasha and Boris were not very reassuring as they tried to outdo each other with their goriest avalanche stories.

We were going nearly vertical now, jabbing our toes into the snow.

'If it slips now we don't stand a chance of coming out alive,' said Boris with what seemed like Slav relish.

We moved one by one. My pulse was pounding. Ahead of us some trees stuck out of the couloir, and I grabbed their branches gratefully, but the gusty wind rocked them and I doubted their roots went deep. On the saddle and without the protection of the mountain the blizzard was even worse. There was no question of going for a summit, whirling snow blotted out everything. The saddle was good enough. Our satisfaction was short lived as we turned to go down.

The storm was now in our faces, the flying flecks of ice like fire on my skin, impossible to use my eyes, I shielded them but couldn't see any way down. Boris and Natasha were hurrying down the steepest bit while I sat and groped for footholds in the icy snow. A fractional lull in the wind brought Natasha's voice, 'No, no, Christina, that is not correct. You must stand upright and dig in your heels.'

To stand on an 80° slope in such a storm, blinded by daggers of ice seemed insane. The wind howled, I leaned into it trying to stand up, it slackened and I nearly tumbled down the ravine. It howled again, I sat and covered my face hoping for another lull. No luck. Somehow I had to go down. Boris and Natasha had gone and their last words were, 'You must hurry, avalanche, God knows.' Lumps of snow and ice dislodged by my feet went hurtling down the abyss. The ice needles were making my eyes so sore that tears poured down my face, freezing on my skin.

At last I got back into the shelter of the lower ravine. The worst was over, and we could allow ourselves to slide down the soft snow slope, laughing and staggering, often falling, knocked over by fierce gusts of wind, our tiredness hardly leaving us the energy to clamber out of the holes we fell in, but we kept laughing. Back at the hut we pulled straws for who would have first turn in the banyo. The bliss of safety.

5

Kronotsky

For the next ten days I was going to join a Russian ranger in Kronotsky Preserve, counting tracks of wild animals and making his rounds on skis. The ranger, Vitali, was reputed to know more about bears than anyone, having spent twenty years studying them. I was very lucky to be going there as Kronotsky is not open to tourists. It is a Preserve not a National Park, and the only people allowed in are the Preserve Administration and guardians such as Vitali. To be invited there one needed to be part of a scientific project, like vulcanologists. Certainly, no foreigner has ever had the privilege of spending ten days there. I made arrangements so that Natasha could come as interpreter and Valentin, a geologist from the south on a sabbatical, would be major-domo.

'Why do I need a major-domo all of a sudden?' I enquired.

'I can frighten the bears,' he replied.

Getting to Kronotsky involved a helicopter. At the airport Natasha told me to keep quiet; she wanted me to pretend to be Russian. Valentin and I swopped coats, me wearing his old darned obviously Russian one and a wool hat to hide my blondness. 'Will you be warm enough?' asked Valentin. So I showed him all my layers of clothing and he said I was like a cabbage. On the passenger list, my name appeared as Katerina Vasilyevna. Natasha had been swotting up her history and filled me in on Kronotsky's origins as we sat in the sun out of earshot of everyone else, waiting for the helicopter. For centuries going back to Ivan the Terrible, the Tsars had levied taxes to be paid in sable furs. In the year 1586 alone, Siberia and the Far East had provided 200,000 sables; 10,000 black foxes and half a million squirrels, beavers and ermines. Furs once accounted for a third of Russia's income, and were called 'soft gold'. So it was hardly surprising that this naturally rich area had been badly exploited, and it was not until 1934 that Kronotsky was given official protected status as a Preserve. Even so, the Valley of Geysers remained undiscovered by Russians until 1941. I pulled out my maps, showing Kronotsky as a mountainous region of nearly 100,000 hectares.

'Why do your maps say Top Secret, and For Military Use Only?' Natasha queried, but I didn't know why.

'They were a gift from Valodya and I don't think they're secret any more.'

Indeed, I had already noticed a marvellous new feeling of openness in Kamchatka. I muffled my camera inside my clothing only to keep it warm and working, not to hide it and no one had minded my taking a photograph of the satellite-tracking station. After all, we all knew a Western satellite camera would already have taken a more useful shot than I could.

It had not always been so and, while we waited for the helicopter we heard booming noises from the military practising inside a nearby extinct volcano. Natasha said her father was a marine officer who had been sent to Kamchatka when she was twelve years old. Then Kamchatka had been closed off from the world, not only because of the plant where nuclear-powered submarines were constructed, but also because it was a target area for the ballistic missile testing programme at Murmansk at the opposite end of the Soviet Union.

'I used to see large missiles with several heads all exploding in the sky at night,' Natasha remembered. 'We also had nuclear bases underground, and radioactive waste which was buried just anywhere. It's now leaking into the rivers. Last year the heavy rains washed more into rivers and there was a public outcry, but nothing was done because we have no anti-radiation containers. To justify having such a large army we were always being told that other countries were planning to attack us. Any unidentified aircraft in our airspace got shot down, like the Korean jet in 1984.'

We boarded our helicopter, along with a two-man delegation from Moldavia on the Romanian border who were coming along for the ride, and flew out past line after line of jet fighter planes inside and outside their camouflaged bunkers. The lookout towers are unmanned nowadays. The outdoor planes had their long mosquito noses and windscreens wrapped up against the cold. Helicopters with double sets of rotor blades, one above the other, were also parked in rows. One flew in above us, moving very fast.

Our flight took us into central Kamchatka and down towards the east coast. The ground was more rugged than in the north, and we could look down into crater lakes, one in particular Vitali said was normally a vivid blue, with its highly poisonous mixture of sulphuric and hydrochloric acid, but at this time of the year it was still frozen, with only a tiny hole of fatal blue in the middle. Kronotsky contains a quarter of all Kamchatka's active volcanoes. It also is known for appalling weather, having intensive cyclones that cause long snowfalls, blizzards, winter storms, and summer rain and fog.

I kept getting electric shocks off the metal of the helicopter, and could see daylight vibrating through the chassis. We circled Kronotsky volcano and headed up a rugged canyon, to be offloaded with our gear in the Valley of Geysers at one of Vitali's huts. Without slackening its rotor, the helicopter hurried away.

The hut was so buried under snow that we had to carve and dig our way to the door before gathering buckets of snow to melt for water. Then I wandered down into the valley. The first geyser I approached was spouting, drenching me in sulphur-smelling spray, so I changed course and found some mud kettles and a mass of hot springs. The whole area seethes with nature's kettles which let off steam as the water temperature comes to the boil. The sun behind me made a circular rainbow in the steam.

Where the ground was warm the snow had melted and emerald-green mosses showed around pink mudflats. Hot iron-coloured rivulets trickled from steaming pools, and rushed down multi-coloured geyserite banks in hot waterfalls. Despite the late sun, my camera kept freezing. I found a way down to the river, ploughed through some snow drifts and crossed the water beside a mesmerising lacy nozzle-shaped fumerole, rambling round entranced until evening.

During supper Vitali told us that when he first came here he was young, silly and lucky. 'I arrived illegally without permit in Kamchatka when I was twenty-eight. Boy, I was such a child then. I took all kinds of jobs; boiler-stoker, driver, fisherman. I had no aim or goal, it was just by chance I came to Kronotsky and was invited to work here as a guardian. I had no other job, so I stayed. That was twenty-four years ago.'

Vitali could not remember his father who went off to the war when he was eight months old in 1938 and was killed in 1945. His mother took no interest in his upbringing or education and he had to learn to look after himself. He left school illiterate. The street friends of his youth were now mostly dead or in prison. Even the Young Pioneers failed to make anything of a young man perfectly willing to be a good Communist. And so he fetched up in Kamchatka and at last found something to which he could devote his life.

He pitched his tent in the valley. At first he hated the loneliness, but after two years he came to terms with the enforced solitude.

'Occasionally I had company when men from the fishing fleet based at Zhupanovo eighty kilometres away would walk here to see the geysers. At that time I was like a protector and guardian of the valley. Then in 1980 there was a fire at Zhupanovo and the base was abandoned. I dismantled the remains of their shacks to make this hut, and found there was enough stuff left to build several more. We'll be staying in some of them over the next ten days.'

In a foggy dawn, at −10°, with frost on the trees, firm crunchy snow underfoot, we set off next morning to accompany Vitali on his work round in the valley. His first task was to check for variation in the geysers. It's hard to know if Geyser Valley is a basin or an ancient collapsed volcanic cone. It seems the water is heated by hot gas, underlain by magma. Vitali said some areas have medicinal springs reputed to alleviate heart and skin troubles, and other springs produce chemicals like carbonic acid, ammonium and bromide.

We crossed the river where icicles hung beside an orange siliceous grotto funnel, and paused to listen to the continual eruption of what Vitali called the Spirit of Water-men. The sound came from large stones bouncing around in the boiling cauldron underground, and it used to be described by the local Itelmen as the talking of spirits. The valley was taboo to them for they believed bad spirits inhabited the geysers, and they never revealed the valley's existence to outsiders.

The indigenous population of southern Kamchatka is not numerous; just a few Kamchadal, Itelmen and Koryaks. The pasture has not enough moss for reindeer. Having no reindeer skins, the Itelmen are reported to have used nettle fibre to make ropes and clothing, for the nettles here grow three metres tall, and sting, but they make a good wrapping, and it is said when fish is wrapped in nettle leaves it doesn't rot for ages.

Fortunately, snow covered the stinging jungle, and we moved easily beside the river and up on to a headland which faced a wall of fiery colour. Vitali likened it to a stained-glass window, and above it was an upper level that spouted cascades of water down the multi-coloured geyserite every half hour. The area was full of exotic nozzles, lips, fountains, a grotto-like pulsating spring, and a tall mouth of gnarled geyserite which had been dead for years, but Vitali made it work to celebrate his fiftieth birthday, by cleaning out the mouth and channel and poking a new hole in it. Now it erupts regularly in spectacular fashion, and he has named it after himself.

Each geyser has its own character and pattern; some have a short interval then a long one between eruptions; in some of them as the water boils it splashes and overflows, others produce flashes of steam. But geysers are rare, since they need a set of very specific circumstances to create them. Hot springs are quite common, the hotter ones may become spouters, and the steam holes are fumeroles. To Vitali's knowledge there have been a few scalded arms and legs when people fall through thin ground into hot springs.

We were on a great open bank of snow watching an eruption and as the steam died away we suddenly heard a helicopter. Our instructions were to run and hide immediately, but we were standing out in the open, easily visible against the snow. We couldn't even hide in the steam.

It seemed our visit really was against the rules. Russian tourists may only fly to Geyser Valley for an hour's stop and not stay overnight or roam in the Preserve as we were. I thought I had obtained permission, but I think it was permission to go in illegally. I'd noticed on the flight in how the pilot flew low behind mountains as if to dodge any possible sighting by Preserve administration.

The helicopter circled us, leaving no doubt we had been seen, and went to land by the hut. Vitali said he would go and talk to them and told us to walk on downriver and keep going so we couldn't be recalled.

We scrambled down past deep rumbling steamy holes called the Gates of Hell, and at the river headed towards a gorge. The water was warm and too deep to cross easily, but we had to keep finding ways to do this as it twisted through the gorge. The rocks underfoot were slimy with dark green weed in which flies were hatching. These warm waters are ideal for certain specifically evolved plants, some unique to Kamchatka, including thermaplants with red rosy flowers, and types of very primitive grasses. Some give animated birth, throwing offshoots like spider plants, instead of propagating by seed. These plants were sent into space for study of their chromosomes and genetic apparatus.

The riverbanks were often smooth steep mud, coloured pink and orange, with emerald-green moss, and above, in complete contrast, icicles hung from banks of snow. While each bend in the river brought a new image of inferno, with rising steam and plumes of vapour.

After several hours and a dozen river crossings the gorge became too tight and we decided to climb out up treacherously steep, slimy clay which clung to our boots. The moss was too weak to support us, as nothing grows very strongly in the gas. It was almost a relief to reach a ravine of snow, but it also slid away under our feet. At the top we circled so the helicopter could not see us. Why was it still there, was it waiting to deport us?

We went over a hill behind the hut and aimed down to a smaller stream. Its water was bath temperature and it led to a five-metre waterfall into a deep pool with steaming hot springs on both sides. As we rambled upstream, listening to the various slow glugging, fast boiling, hissing, spitting sounds from the springs, I revelled in the colours of the earth, and the trees still covered in frost.

Mid-afternoon when the helicopter took off, we hid by some rocks, then feeling ravenous, went back to Vitali's hut. To our amusement we learned the helicopter was also visiting illegally, and had merely stopped in for lunch and, less amusing, they had eaten ours!

'Never mind,' said Vitali, 'I am the best cook in this part of

Kamchatka,' and he tipped oil into a pan to fry some onions. Strange oil, it evaporated without browning the onions. He added more. It wasn't oil and God knows what it was, but the meal tasted great. After lunch we explored the shallow hollows where Vitali said bears lie and doze on summer days. A major part of his work, and the part for which he is well known, is his study of brown bears. The Kamchatka bear, said to be the world's largest with a maximum weight of 700 kilos, looks much the same as the American brown bear or grizzly. The only difference is in the configuration of the skull, the grizzly has a broader jaw, and of course the diet is different. Lacking the equipment available to American researchers, like homing devices on collars, Vitali has to do his field work the hard way, by marching around, observing, taking photographs, and making notes, identifying the bears by individual characteristics, and giving them nicknames. He was a bit like a bear himself with his curly ruff of reddish-grey beard and shaggy mane of hair, stocky and probably aggressive if threatened.

'Once I saw a bear lying against the end of a snow drift, using the snow as a pillow. It was twenty metres away, and looked like the bear I called Athlete, so I went closer. I was sure he could hear my steps but he made no reaction, I went closer still and took some photos, his body filled the frame. Then I coughed and with the speed of sound the bear jumped up and bounded at me. At four metres he stood up on his back legs. I dropped everything except my revolver, which I fired into the air. The bear stood immobile, I fired again. Then at the same moment we both turned and ran, fortunately in different directions.

'Another day I was attacked by a female bear on a slope. I fell, she chased after me and also fell. As we tumbled down she rolled over me twice. Her weight nearly flattened me. She went on rolling, I managed to scramble back uphill, very bruised.

'We're now at the end of the hibernation period, and when

we go touring this week I'll be counting their tracks to tell how many have woken up.'

A small white animal with black-tipped tail scurried past, an ermine, hunting for an evening meal. We watched it scamper along the stream bank and jump over rivulets of hot water, stopping to inspect all holes for possible supper. In summer the ermines become chocolate-brown colour. They don't hibernate, neither does their food supply of mice. Vitali said that once by accident he had brought some rats to his hut, hidden in food supplies. At first he was puzzled to see rat traces because there are no rats in Kronotsky, but his stored bedding was chewed to shreds, then he saw one near his supplies and realised what had happened.

'Curiously, I'd brought only rats of one sex and they went crazy trying to find mates. When they went out of the hut to search farther afield, I saw their tracks, and the tracks of the ermine that ate them one by one. Ermines don't become a pest like rats because they don't store food, they just eat what they want at that moment. There's an ermine living near the hut. It's better than a cat, a really quick beast of prey with a strong hunting instinct.'

In the morning we donned backpacks and cross-country skis, and, having closed up the hut and said goodbye to the geysers, we set off up a tributary valley. Ahead of us lay a long climb up into a tall mountain range. Our tributary had gas holes that became fewer until the snow took over entirely. At first we climbed wearing skis, making duck-steps to get a grip.

We passed within four kilometres of Death Valley. Vitali goes there occasionally to remove the dead animals.

'It's not really a valley, more like a small canyon with several brooks in it. The place looks entirely normal, there's nothing to warn you, though sometimes you can smell the gas.

'There's different death points where gases escape. The killer is hydrogen sulphide. Most deaths happen mid-June. A bear takes a long time to die. Weather conditions affect the speed of death. If there's a wind the poison is diluted, but if the day is windless and foggy I feel its effect on me within a couple of minutes. I can't breathe, I think there's no air. It feels as if your mouth and nose are shut.'

The day was gloriously sunny with no wind, the snow dazzling white on the peaks soaring ahead of us. From couloir to couloir, we climbed up and up, with no danger of avalanche, since it was much colder here. I lost sight of the others, Vitali had gone ahead, Natasha, being an expert on skis, was close behind him; I was ambling happily in their wake, with Valentin far behind because he was unused to skis and was carrying the heaviest pack. I enjoyed the swish of my skis and watched two eagles gliding above.

At the base of a steep old avalanche we took off our skis and began the major part of the climb, an hour's hard work up the avalanche, stabbing our toes in for footholds. The view from the top was breathtaking, extending to the volcano called Uzon with its hidden crater lake. Uzon was a mighty spirit who lived on the summit and, according to legend, helped mankind by closing volcano craters with his powerful hands when they were about to erupt. He also pacified giant wild deer and did many good deeds but he lived alone and was not allowed to show anyone his home because of a taboo by wicked spirits, or kalau. Uzon longed for human company, and a council of good spirits decided to allow him to choose a wife in the nearby camp of nomads.

So he wandered invisibly until he fell in love with a beauty named Nayun, and took her back to his volcano where they lived very happily for many years. Eventually Nayun began pining for human contact and asked Uzon to let her visit her relatives. Kindly Uzon could not refuse her request. With his great hands he moved apart the mountains and a road appeared for Nayun to walk down. Soon Uzon heard noises.

It was people coming on Nayun's road to see him. The kalau's taboo was violated, mountains shook, there was a terrible noise as the earth yawned, devouring the summit, and mighty Uzon was turned to stone for ever in a sad pose with bowed head. Real tears poured from the stone eyes of this rocky hero in the form of a noisy river. Now the wicked kalau live in the crater, stirring malicious gases and poisons but Uzon's tears cool and make them harmless. So Uzon continues to serve people long after his death.

For several kilometres the gradient was gentle, heading towards a hilly region with long promontories stretching away like fingers, dotted with birch trees. The descent was steep in parts. I tried to zigzag but the skis had no bite on the hillside. It was already afternoon, and for three or four hours we descended, as gradually as we could.

I crossed the week-old tracks of a bear and a more recent wolverine. My shoulders were aching from the pack, and whenever I fell it was hard to get up. We all fell and no one waited to help anyone else, though I hung back to keep an eye on Valentin's struggles. Vitali's pace was steady, it didn't even slacken when he skiied through bushes. But I had noticed him limping occasionally the day before and he admitted he'd been shot in the leg years ago by a poacher.

'I couldn't imagine why he did it. His offence as a drunk poacher was trifling until he fired at me. Then he reloaded his shotgun and told me, "I'm going to kill you to death." There I was lying on the ground with my leg hanging off, it was like being in an American western. I tried to reason with him but he raised the gun and aimed it at me. So I pulled out my revolver and shot him first in the neck. He didn't fall, so I fired again into his groin. He turned to run, my third bullet got him in the buttocks. I wished I'd had more bullets. We were rescued, taken to hospital and the poacher went to prison for eight years.

'I had trouble because the first doctor threatened to amputate my leg, so I changed doctors and I recovered. But the broken leg was seven centimetres shorter. I used an apparatus to lengthen it, but it's still a tad short.'

He certainly showed no stiffness on skis, and had vanished, leaving me alone again. The easy slopes were great for gliding along. I saw where a bear had slid down one, then rolled and padded away. His prints were larger than both of my feet put together.

We traversed two more valleys before we finally reached Vitali's Number Two hut. He had stoked the fire, boiled the kettle, and cleared snow from the door before we arrived, and we were all so hungry we made a giant pot of rice. For the first course we had rice and meat sauce, then rice and dried milk, rice and sugar, and rice mixed with sweet tea.

Vitali told us about the time he arrived to find the door ajar.

'I don't ever lock my huts but I do close them properly against the wind. I walked cautiously up to it and listened. There was a noise but as I went to peep through the door it closed. So I stood on an upturned crate and peered in through a window. At that very moment the intruder moved to the same window and glared back at me – a bear, and since it had inadvertently pushed the door shut, it was trapped inside.'

Eventually, the bear smashed its way out but not before it had created chaos, eating foodstuffs, clawing at the windows, and scratching away all the insulation. Vitali showed us its toothmarks. The year before, he had arrived at the hut to find a window broken.

'It wasn't until I walked around and caught sight of my reflection in the windows that I understood what had happened. A bear had come up, seen his reflection and thought it was a rival.'

These bear stories did not make for the best of nights. Added to which I had to wear all my clothes for, although the hut had mattresses, they were damp and the cold seeped into me.

The skiing was great next morning. As before, Vitali had vanished far ahead saying, 'Follow my tracks,' Natasha was close behind him, and Valentin way back. After an hour I swung round a corner to see a large brown bear come sliding down the valley side. We were on a collision course, although he didn't appear to have seen me. I braked hard, snow-ploughing up the side of a knoll, trying to keep out of his sight. Was he going to see me, smell me, hear me? I froze.

The bear was now standing on Vitali's ski tracks, his dark brown fur very shaggy. Which way would he go? It wasn't worth feeling afraid, either the bear would come my way or it wouldn't. Vitali's idea that bears were not hungry yet didn't tie up with him saying male bears are particularly aggressive in the mating season. I stayed still but slid out of my pack for a quick escape. The biggest danger would be if Valentin caught up and came down the valley in his usual out-of-control and unstoppable way. I got ready to wave warnings at him.

In a twist of amusement I thought if the bear went down the track ahead of me I'd also be in a predicament. Should I try to build up enough speed to whizz past him? While I waited and watched, the bear began to pick his way up the opposite side of the valley, great paws sinking deep, his head not turning to look, not aware of the turbulent emotions he was causing. He kept going, ploughing slowly uphill, pausing occasionally but not in alarm. When I reckoned that he was out of pouncing distance I put my back pack on, still no sign of Valentin, it was time to move on.

A mile later I found Natasha waiting for me beside two great holes scratched in the snow. She said Vitali had wanted to tell me about this place. One hole was where two bears had fought some time ago, a long fearsome fight to the death. The struggle marks were still there, gashes on trees showing the ferocity of their rivalry displays. When Vitali originally found this place the dead bear was lying disembowelled and picked over by scavengers. It had been about twenty years old, weighing 350 kilos, matched against a smaller bear which had gained an advantage because it poked out the larger bear's eye.

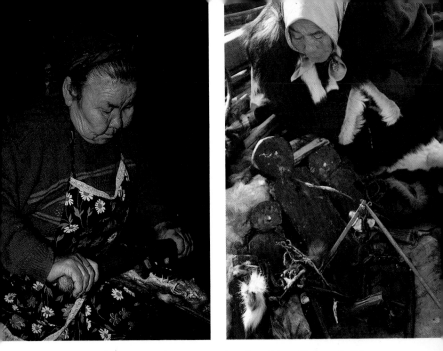

Above left, Makar's wife Hilin, scrapes deer-leg skin with her obsidian flint; *above right,* Koryak totems which work for the family wellbeing; *below left,* children are dressed like plump furry animals, complete with the original ears. My namesake, Christina, is in the middle; *below right,* a Koryak herder.

Above left: Larissa, star of the bottom-waggling seal ballet. *Above right,* the magic toadstool sketch was always popular. *Below,* 'Rhythm of the Tundra'. Drums are an important part of Koryak ritual and dance.

The Beringei dog-sled race: *above left,* the Russian from Chukotka who was way ahead of the field; *above right,* the first racers arriving at Palana; *below,* the start line after a twenty-four hour delay for sobering up.

Above, Provodizimai, the holiday to celebrate the end of winter, brings out the inhabitants of Palana. *Below,* Big Taya, in black, at Tanya the dentist's birthday party.

The volcanic backbone of central Kamchatka.

In the Valley of Geysers.

Above, Kronotsky Preserve: Vitali's Number Four hut near the coast.
Below left, negotiating a snow bridge. *Below right*, Valentin hated skis.

The Easter picnic on the beach at Korf.

Above left, The Little King waits for his transport to be repaired. *Above right,* Tungan prepares pantui from young deer antlers. Despite appearances, it was a great delicacy. *Below,* her daughter rubs fat on the Chukchi family totems.

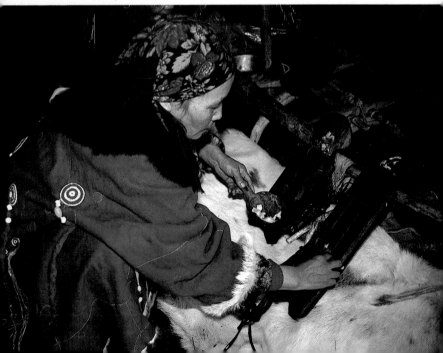

The second great hole in the snow was made just a few days ago when the victorious bear returned and picked up the scent of the dead bear lying under the snow. Bears often bury or cache surplus food, and don't mind eating putrid meat.

This year the smaller bear would have been about 350 kilo judging by his prints, which Valentin, who had now arrived, measured as nineteen centimetres wide. From the fresh tracks leading away in the direction we had come the bear would undoubtedly have been the one I met. Yes, I agreed, it had looked big to me, too.

All morning we had been gradually working around the base of a jagged collapsed volcano and, when we rounded this, we headed for the classical cone of the volcano from which the Preserve takes its name. With a star-shaped glacier on its summit, making tongues down radial couloirs, Kronotsky is now blocked at the top. The side facing us had several active cinder cones. But its activity is mounting once more and at present it is in an intermediate stage before another possible major summit eruption.

We came out on to a great plain from which rose Krasheninnikov, a double volcano in a vast caldera. Where Vitali's tracks entered woodland the rest of us stopped and raided Valentin's pack for lunch, dry bread only. I put snow on mine to make snow sandwiches. We looked darkly at Vitali's ski tracks, mentally preparing ourselves for another six kilometres. But when we crossed a stream we saw the hut, flying a faded pink flag.

I was becoming intrigued by Vitali's huts, each so self-contained, and each stamped with the character of their builder. Over the years he had had many fights with the administration who forbade him to build huts, but he paid no attention. He says he doesn't fight with them, they fight with him. His position is also unique because of his lack of academic qualifications. But because they need his experience and expertise they have made a special case by giving him the title of Scientific Assistant.

This was Vitali's favourite hut, with a study tacked on the sunny side, which he gave to me and Natasha as a bedroom. He lit a second stove and we had the luxury of a banyo, pouring mugfuls of hot water over ourselves. Natasha covered herself in soap, saying, 'Russian soap is the best in the world because it has no chemicals, it's only made of fat.'

I wasn't convinced that smearing soapy grease was the best. Would it follow that Russian coffee is the best because it has no coffee in it? She laughed and agreed to concede the point.

The walls of Vitali's study were full of books, on biology, history, geography, philosophy, poetry. Vitali said the greatest Russian poet Pushkin had just started writing about the land of Kamchatka when he died in a duel over his wife's honour. There was a dictionary of Russian etymology and a full shelf of encyclopaedia, which Vitali claimed he had read, plus the complete works of Lenin. He suggested perhaps Lenin had simply cribbed ideas from the Bible.

The writer who particularly interested me was Krasheninnikov, who became Russia's first native botanist, travelling to Kamchatka with Bering in 1738 and roaming the peninsula for four years without salary or support, collecting information on plants and minerals, sea and land mammals, birds, and peoples; he also gathered historical data and studied legends and languages of the natives for his book *Description of the Land of Kamschatka* published in 1755.

A rare white-shouldered eagle took off from a tree outside the door. With its big yellow hooked beak and a wingspan of over two metres, it is larger than both the golden and the bald eagle. Vitali pointed to its nest nearby and said it lived there for three months each year. Usually two eggs hatch, and one of the chicks kills the other in order to get all the food, it's the survival of the greediest.

Built in the loop of a river that never freezes, the hut shares a huge skyline with snowy volcanoes. In the late afternoon sun we donned skis again and went rambling along the river-bank. Vitali pointed out where a wolverine had bounded along in soft snow making deep hollows with all four legs, and later, when the snow was firm, had trotted back leaving clear shallow paw marks. His tracks were later crossed by a fox sniffing around, then by a partridge, and further on we found the remains of the wings of a young white-shouldered eagle caught by a wolverine. Vitali said the young tend to be caught if they are fishing in the river and their feathers get too soaked for flight when the wolverine pounces. Tracks showed that after the wolverine's feast the fox had turned up and finished all but the feathers.

At the head of the river was a lake with springs in it which sent the water rippling out in concentric waves. Six swans were calling musically as they flew along the river's course. We ambled back through woodlands and over an exposed plain, able to see the detail of a volcanic pre-caldera massif. Kronotsky's cone was still lit by sunshine. It was the time of year the Russians call 'Spring of Light' because the days grow longer and are sunny. Animals become more active, tree buds grow larger but won't open until early June. Next is May, called 'Spring of Water' when snow starts to melt. This was a cue for another of Vitali's slightly surreal stories.

'A house I lived in fell down in the spring melt, when I was just a child,' he recalled. 'My family lived on a riverbank above Tbilisi and my mother left me as usual locked indoors alone. In the mudslide half the building broke away and slid into the river. I heard screams as people ran outside. The floor under me began to tilt. A window opened and my grandfather stretched out his hand to me. He was slightly mad, having been in prison for many years, but he put out his hand and, as I grasped it, the room split open. The noise and dust were ter-rible, and as they cleared I saw that where the wall had been was now a wonderful panorama of hills and greenery. That's partly why, in the buildings I make, I put as many south-facing windows as possible, to get the impression of having no south wall.'

I sat outside drinking tea on the bear barricades; big logs surrounding the hut so the bears can't tear at the timbers and the weatherproof bitumen felt. Vitali described the bear's warning signs of nodding its head to the ground, or swinging it from side to side. When a bear roars it uses all the force of its neck and vocal cords and when it charges, he said, it gallops on all fours, ears flattened back and its mouth in a round 'O'.

Vitali questioned me about the bear I had met, to know if it was the fighting bear of last year, and Valentin confirmed the large fresh tracks he had seen that were not there when Vitali skied down. I thought maybe the bear had heard Vitali, moved away, and slid down into my path. It had certainly been a sight sliding on its bottom. Vitali said that was quite normal at this time of year, since it helps loosen the bear's constipated system. He said I should have climbed a tree if charged. Only small bears can climb trees, after the age of three they become too heavy and their claws cannot support their weight.

The evening's talk was all about Vitali's experience of observing bears. A sow has two or three cubs, a maximum of five, which Vitali has seen only once in twenty years. New-born cubs are blind, naked, toothless, and about the size of the palm of your hand, weighing from fifty grams to a kilo. They are born while the mother is still asleep in her winter hibernation and their instincts start them suckling.

In spring young bears flirt with each other, struggling and wrestling, biting each others' necks and legs, rolling over and chasing around. This is the only time when a female can afford to beat a male. Adult bears are solitary and wander long distances in search of food and to mate. They are not exclusive about territory. However, small bears run when a larger bear wants their space. Young have no established fishing spots, they rely on stealing off the old. Vitali described the look of mischievous impudence when a youngster steals from an elder whose back is turned.

A bear's lifespan is twenty to thirty-five years, and they usually die when their teeth fall out. Elsewhere they can live for fifty years but in Kronotsky the weather conditions are too severe for longevity. About four hundred bears live within the Preserve, their population naturally stabilised by the harsh conditions. However, big males will kill cubs if there are too many, and quite often eat them, not from hunger, said Vitali, but out of aggression.

I slept in a dog-fur sleeping-bag, nicely warm as I'd thought I should be, since dogs sleep contentedly outside.

Through the windows I could see the full moon rise, but later it disappeared into a thick mass of cloud which didn't bode well for the next day's weather.

It dawned grey. Vitali and I went looking for bears' winter dens, up a broad valley between low thickets of alder bushes. As autumn snow builds up and forces the bushes to bend over, the trapped air spaces make ideal dens. Bears do not hibernate in the true sense of the word, since there is no dramatic drop in body temperature and heart rate. When a bear sleeps it is in fairly continual movement, shifting around and scratching its fur, often sucking its claws. The fur it swallows off its claws provides a little action for the stomach, and the furballs clog the lower intestine and act as a plug so the den is kept clean. Itelmen myths say that hibernating bears can read people's thoughts.

We picnicked at a fallen tree Vitali dubbed Birchtree Café and by late afternoon we had looped back across a glorious open plain flanked by volcanoes and lakes.

It snowed heavily all night, which pleased Vitali since it would cover our tracks and conceal the fact we had been all over the place. It was still snowing lightly in the morning, certainly not enough to put off our plans. We were intending to go fifteen kilometres along the coast. Soon Vitali was a distant blur in the falling snow. There were no landmarks, just the white empty land under a leaden sky.

Gradually I could hear the roar of the ocean. We skied over

what may have been sand dunes and found ourselves by the sea. Snow lay to the high tide mark, the beach of black volcanic sand was steaming because it was warmer than the falling snow. White waves were rolling in, I took off my skis and went down to feel the water temperature. About 5°. Two snouts appeared in the waves, inquisitive fur seals, who watched us as we loaded our skis on to our packs, in order to walk beside the sea.

The tideline was one of the cleanest I have seen, with no man-made rubbish, just a few coloured stones, shells, lacy kelp, and what eagles had left of a crab. Our steps covered miles on that wonderfully desolate beach, white snow falling on black sand edged by white waves.

Hills became visible, we left the beach, put on skis, and Vitali said I should follow his tracks closely as we were going across a rather treacherous lagoon. Its surface was lumpy and pitted with old ice, but Vitali never wavered. Beyond it we crossed a river on an old wooden bridge built by poachers, and later crossed again on two angled logs. In mid-afternoon we climbed into the hills and there at the top of one hill was Vitali's fourth hut, overlooking many miles of coast in both directions.

It is a natural lookout point, and there had been an Itelmen village here three hundred years ago. I could see small mounds where their huts had once stood, and Vitali told me he had found stone axes and stone knives used for cleaning fish and game. Yes, one could live very happily here, easily defended, the river below, abundant fish, sea mammals, hunting. The Itelmen community who lived here weren't destroyed by enemies, they were wiped out by an epidemic of smallpox, very likely brought in by the Russians and fur traders. Along with the Itelmen, almost a quarter of all Chukchi, Eskimo and Eveni perished in the 1899 epidemic.

We had one lazy day at Hut Four while a blizzard raged. It was quite pleasant to relax, with plenty of food and firewood, talking about life, hopes and fears, though Vitali was a bit like a caged animal. In quieter moments he talked about his life and work, his copious notes and diaries, and his photo collection which must be one of the largest studies of bears ever made.

'My work is a task I fear I'll never complete. When I'm working, I'm satisfied; the process is more important than the result.'

When the blizzard subsided we left our skis and walked by the waves, crashing rollers foaming in and hitting banks of ice. A river ran parallel to the beach, and on the bank we saw fresh bear tracks, then we saw the bear itself, sitting watching us from the far bank. It felt safe, and we felt safe, so we stared at each other. Its great shaggy coat rippled and shimmered as it shook its head. Then it folded its front legs and lay down to continue surveillance. We walked on and Natasha entertained us with a story she'd wanted to tell me earlier, about a friend called Fedor who counted bears in southern Kamchatka. One spring he went to a remote hut he'd closed up the previous autumn. The door was battered but closed, and inside he found a dead bear which had got itself trapped and looked as if it had died of starvation. The only clue was a hand towel which had once been bright red. Now it lay like a white sausage on the floor. There had been no food in the hut, the trapped bear had eaten the only thing it could find. Inside the bear's stomach the towel had been bleached white by the stomach enzymes before being excreted. After removing the bear, Natasha said, Fedor washed the towel and hung it up again in its usual place, which says something about the scarcity of consumer goods in Russia! Vitali snored so loudly in the night I resorted to my helicopter earplugs. He snored like a bear, except he didn't suck his claws.

Between Vitali's Number Four and Number Five huts the going got tougher and we struggled forward over two low ridges. An occasional red ribbon on a branch was a trailmark so Vitali could find his way in fog or blizzard. He had also cut notches in his walking boots so he could tell his own tracks from those of possible poachers.

We trekked through light taiga, over plains and across swamps weaving between melting pockets in the snow. In these grow marsh grasses, one of the first bear foods in the spring and there were also masses of poisonous carrot-like floating tubers called Tsikuta. Vitali says that was what killed the Greek philosopher Socrates and suggested that Kamchatka could export poison to any country which suffers from a surfeit of philosophers!

We were now heading back to Hut Three, my favourite, and that evening when I failed to find World Service news on the radio we heard speeches from the National Congress in Moscow. The speaker for Kamchatka ranted and raved, enumerating problems, then taking off at a tangent about vodka and never putting forward any solutions. This was the Congress of which the reindeer-herders had such high hopes. The speeches went on all night, for noon in Moscow is nine o'clock in the evening in Kamchatka. Nine time zones away, it made me realise the vastness of Russia. I curled up in the dog-fur sleeping-bag and dozed.

The weather next day began to turn foul again and we only covered twelve kilometres. Our errand was to collect a bag of chaga fungus which grows as a bulging black scab on the trunks of certain trees. It is sold in Petropavlovsk as medicine for liver complaints and against the first stages of cancer. I was intrigued by the icicles that built up on Vitali's moustache. Natasha came up with the Russian saying: not even a dog owner would let his dog out in such weather. Vitali responded with the adage: there's no such thing as bad weather, only bad clothes. To make us count our blessings he told us the region we were skiing over was impassable in summer because the grasses and bushes grow so tall that even the bears have a struggle to create paths and tunnels through. And with leaves on the trees you can never see very far. As for mosquitoes, in summer the whole of Kamchatka and Siberia is buzzing with large hungry hordes. So on the whole I was thankful to be in sub-zero snow and not encumbered with a mossie hat and veil. At two p.m. we came to a lake and great flocks of duck and snipe wheeled in the air. To help me identify the types of birds and animals I had a photocopied page of Krasheninnikov with translations. It caused amusement when the others spotted a misprint. For cuckoo the book had printed *kokashke*. It should be *kukushke*; the other word means shit.

On the edge of the lake was Hut Six, so tiny that Vitali said he didn't count it among his eight. The barricades had been mauled by a bruin, the door posts were freshly chewed, the door planks scratched by claws, and the tarred felt was torn away in chunks, not because the bear was trying to get in, but as a statement to let it be known that the hut was on his territory, so had received his mark.

On our final day I got up early to ski down to the ocean for a last glimpse of the swirling sea fog, whipped on by the surf under the wild flying sky. Kronotsky had been ten days of exhilaration I would never forget.

6

Into Volcano Country

After spending ten days waiting for Valentin to catch up with Vitali it was an interesting change to travel with him at his own pace in the part of southern Kamchatka where he worked as a geologist. Valentin claimed to speak a bit of French but, since he had never embarked on a French conversation before, it was more confusing than helpful. So, at first, I still relied largely on Natasha's somewhat erratic interpreting.

'They are going to shoot you,' she informed me urgently one day as a posse of men bore down on us with intent. But it was only a local television crew, keen to enlist the visiting foreigner in the debate about the proposed Southern Kamchatka National Park. The area was agreed. Even Yeltsin was said to be 'in accord', but he had offered no material assistance, and the Moscow institute which deals with national parks, the Scientific Institute of Nature Protection, have no power except to make recommendations. They had approved the proposal two years ago.

The twenty-thousand-square-kilometres area took in the whole of southern Kamchatka below Petropavlovsk. It included over one hundred hot springs and an impressive variety of animal, bird and plant life, some of it unique to Kamchatka and a good proportion of protected rare species.

As yet there were no roads and few villages in the entire southern peninsula.

'But,' as one of the disillusioned campaigners said to me, 'doubtless in the end the area will be used for mining gold, silver, building materials and anything exploitable.'

The presenter from the TV company joined us for supper; she said the last time she had the chance to meet a foreigner, she had been too embarrassed to allow him into her house. Her fifteen-year-old daughter had asked if she could bring a visiting American student home with her, but her mother knew the fridge was empty and the house had no carpet, and she was too ashamed to say yes. She said she had cried all night.

Despite drinking a lot of vodka, in the evening I got the chance to do some washing. Valentin had an ancient twin tub. He said, 'Turn this knob, keep your foot on that hose so water doesn't spray out, and hold the lid like this to make the cylinder spin.'

'I see, and use your free foot to stand on,' I rejoined. It worked fine until I stopped concentrating on what I was supposed to be doing with my arms and legs and half the soapy tub emptied itself into the spin-drying part. To Valentin a defective Russian washing-machine was just symptomatic of a greater failure. He saw things in black and white and in his opinion all intelligent people were wiped out during Stalin's purges. Anyone with ambition or education, even farmers who had worked hard to prosper, were sent to prisons. Only people too stupid and lazy to be a threat were left. 'Is it any surprise that our leaders are incompetent.'

To my mind, a lot of reforms were simply being blocked by bureaucrats at all levels because change threatened the security of their jobs. And it seemed to me that Russians in general enjoyed grumbling. 'There are a million millionaires in America,' they would wail. 'Why can't we be rich, too?'

I would reply that reality is struggle, and berate them for wanting everything on a plate, and blaming the state when things went wrong.

Valentin often complained about poverty, yet for ten years he and his family had taken a three-month holiday every year, flying up to ten thousand kilometres. I said, 'No Westerner can afford that kind of life. Boy, you had it good.'

Valentin took my robust response in good part. In his spare time he cultivated an acre of vegetables every year, spreading ash from the fire over the snow to help it melt a couple of weeks earlier in the painfully short growing season. The land is not fertile, as one would expect from the volcanic activity. Valentin went technical about types of lava being acid or alkaline; most of Kamchatka's volcanoes are acid, being very young andesite-basalt, and instead of fine silt the grains are coarse and large. I had read a Communist book that spoke of great agricultural developments planned in Kamchatka, using volcanic ash to fertilise fields. 'Rubbish,' Valentin said, 'all rubbish.'

By now Natasha had a job elsewhere, so Valentin and I set off for the Mutnofski volcano region with another Russian ski champion-interpreter called Luda, in the back of a geology truck. The gravel road soon deteriorated into muddy snowy ruts as we approached the narrow defile known as the Gates to the South. Great banks of snow towered higher than the truck on either side. By mid-day the track was high among volcanoes and mountains, marked by poles at every thirty metres, so drivers would not lose their way. We could see pillars of steam from inside Mutnofski crater and other jets billowing from snowy hillsides.

The main resources of the Mutnofski thermal belt are boiling water and steam. There is estimated to be enough steam power to generate electricity for the whole of Petropavlovsk a hundred kilometres away.

At the office of the geologists' camp there were charts showing the current drilling. Their deepest holes went down 2,500 metres, with the hazard that when they hit very hot water under pressure, it could boil up the borehole with increasing fury, and the eruption of steam at the top would make the pressure drop, sometimes forcing the shaft to collapse. They had used oil-drilling equipment for exploratory work because, as Valentin explained, it has a smaller drill diameter for taking samples. On one occasion the pressure shot the drill out of its hole to hit the crown block on top of the rig with such force that it twisted and curled like a piece of spaghetti.

We continued to the main camp at Dachny where Valentin had been working. He was still employed by the company, but like many of his colleagues expected to be laid off before long. First we visited the hot springs, then some new boreholes, all dwarfed in the enormous bleak emptiness. One roaring giant jet was three metres across at its base and threw a pillar of steam thirty metres into the air. Its borehole was over a thousand metres deep.

Valentin's colleagues gave him a boisterous welcome. These Russians liked their self-imposed exile. They seemed to be people who would not fit well among the conforming majority in central Russia; they were loners, too independent, self-reliant, and strong willed to fit a mould. Their nature, like the climate, went to extremes. Valentin was in his element and seemed taller. One of his colleagues called Valodya told me about the days when brave and dashing young geologists used to form cliques, calling themselves Hussars. To qualify you had to be able to drink to oblivion yet still fire a rifle accurately.

'Whenever we had an argument we would solve it by a type of duel. One party would balance an empty glass on his head, and the other would shoot it off from a distance of fifteen metres. They they would swap turns.'

'Did you have a glass shot off your head?'

'Yes often. Some mornings I'd wake up with my hair full of splintered glass. We did it frequently, and when very drunk, but I can't remember any deaths.'

Then he went on, 'Another man, Vasia, a Hungarian engineer who was deprivileged six times for professional misconduct, was finally reinstated and returned to the camp, but we wouldn't let him rejoin the Hussars. He was so upset he forced his way into our hut and, wearing just his felt boots, he danced on top of the hot stove. His boots began to smoulder. We poured water into them. But he wouldn't come down until we had agreed to let him rejoin the club.

'In those days our units were run on gulag prison camp lines, since most of our labour force was ex-prisoners. The men who lived to leave gulags were either very strong or very broken. Most simply settled nearby because they had nowhere else to go. We used to employ them because they were not allowed to seek work in towns and we felt sorry for them. Most were ex-criminals, they often threatened to kill us. The unit couldn't be run on Communist lines of equality for all. We were a bunch of qualified engineers. So we ran it as a gulag to keep order and maintain authority.'

Prisoners could be criminals, or political exiles. In Stalin's time anything was enough to warrant banishment. As well as waves of war prisoners and criminals, there was a massive number of political convicts who never stood trial but whose existence was 'prejudicial to public order or incompatible with public tranquillity'. The administrative order that allowed this was a disgrace to Russia. Petty officials had the power to banish people to Siberia without giving a reason. Paying off grudges was easy. Sometimes it took four years for the convicts to reach their destination, and half of the chained ones died en route. In the fifty years after the government began keeping records, 772,979 prisoners and exiles were sent into these wastelands. Some sources put the number a lot higher. There were prison camps dotted everywhere, often located near mines to provide mine labourers. The largest camp had 35,000 inmates.

Valentin's grandfather was sent to prison, his wife and three children never knew what happened to him, nor why he was sent. He had been awarded three Communist Party stars for good work, then was arrested and imprisoned for life. Valentin's uncle later tried to find out why, but no records had been kept.

Luda and I retired to get ready for a banyo. Luda's family came to Kamchatka because her grandfather was exiled. Again there was no reason. In was in 1905 after a failed revolution against the Tsar. At that time nearly 100,000 political prisoners were sent east and even Siberia had trouble absorbing them all. Some of these exiles became famous, like the beautiful Anna Korba who agitated for peasant education and was sent to the Siberian mines for twenty years' hard labour; and Madame Breshkovskaya, an outspoken teacher who was condemned for twenty-two years and trekked on foot for three thousand kilometres across the Arctic.

Lenin spent three years in Siberia but was lucky to be given a log cabin where he could study, write, make long hunting trips, and prepare for his life's work. Stalin was banished to Siberia six times, and each time escaped to continue his revolutionary work. He was a sickly type when he was first exiled, but was cured by Siberia's bracing climate and, like Lenin, benefited from time to study the socialist classics. Instead of smothering the revolutionaries, exile brought them into bloom.

A fair number of exiles were highly qualified people, some had specialist knowledge in the sciences, and were permitted to use their talents in Siberia, bringing to Russia a better understanding of these eastern wastelands. But the land was also a dumping-ground for Russia's seriously undesirables. Tens of thousands escaped from prisons, few were recaptured, though Siberia and the Far East were a natural prison by reason of their remoteness. The hard-labour convict was legally dead, losing all rights over children and wife. She could accompany him if she wished, or remarry as if he were dead. Luda's grandmother accompanied her husband to Siberia, where he lived as a hunter. Luda's mother was born in 1924 in Omsk-Kamchatka, the town based on Kamchatka's largest political-prisoner gulag. Her father came to Kamchatka from the Ukraine as an infantry sergeant, and Luda was also born in Omsk-Kamchatka which is still a military centre.

As well as an indoor banyo, there was a natural banyo on a hillside where Luda and I took our bath, climbing down through the snow to ground level, four metres below. The pool was fed by a hot stream and had a tunnel created by the hot outflow with a point of light at the far end of the tunnel where it emerged further down the hill. There was the usual spade provided for shovelling snow to cool you down.

Some of the mineral waters are medicinal for heart trouble, lumbago, and skin diseases. Luda lay soaking for a long time, to get full benefit from the banyo. Her intense athletic training during fifteen years as a top skier had had a bad effect on her health, and at thirty she was told that if she didn't retire from competitive sport she could soon die of a heart attack. She said Russian athletes often retire with broken health when they have trained beyond their physical limits. Now she was unemployed.

At night it was strange to sleep with the eerie roaring of boreholes outside my window sounding like a jet aircraft warming up for take-off.

Though he had worked here for eight years Valentin had never been inside Mutnofski crater, so next day we decided to find the way in through a dangerously avalanche-prone canyon. In its upper reaches we had to cross a steeply plunging glacier. One false step and you would hurtle down the canyon with no hope of stopping. The first thing I saw as we entered the crater was a field of ice pillars about seven metres tall standing among and over a series of steam vents. The steam makes the pillars grow at night when the air temperature drops below freezing. In the morning sun they glistened blue and green. The most recently active part of the crater had formed a new semi-caldera inside the main one. The outer caldera was seething with hot springs encrusted in violent yellow sulphur crystals, and we coughed in clouds of sulphur steam and poisonous ammonium chloride. The ground grew hot and soggy in places, forcing us to test it with our ski poles and back off where it was clearly unsafe. Caverns were visible through cracks in the bilious yellow rock. Tall yellow chimneys poked up, noisily hissing and spluttering. Parts of the ground were covered in a surface of calcium, magnesium, sodium and potassium sulphate. A big round pool of seething thick grey-brown sludge gurgled and spouted. Nearby a hot ochre-yellow stream ran between mauve banks.

To reach the new and most active crater we climbed for an hour up a great bank of ice and snow, then used a rope to pull ourselves up and on to the rim where we perched, awestruck, on a thin crumbly ledge above a vertical 200-metre drop into the steam-filled crater which, hissing and billowing, obliterated all view.

The view as we skied back was breathtaking. What stretched ahead to every horizon was an empty mass of crystalline peaks, piercing deep blue sky and curving down into desolate valleys. I gazed at them in wonder in between judging my turns around black cinder cones and volcanic bombs, making my tentative snowploughs with bursts of speed on short steep sections from shoulder to shoulder as we made for the lower slopes.

Valentin wanted to show us where he had worked at the drill rig and because it had been shut down we were able to climb up into it, past the huge generators, the stacks of borehole pipes, and old drill heads with metal studded triple paws to gyrate and chew into rock. He told us about the early days and the explosions that happened while they were learning how to manage the drilling.

'One time I had calculated that at 200 metres the water temperature would be 200°C. In order to stop the soft earth falling into the hole you have to put in a preventor to hold things secure. We knew it should sit at 150 metres but we hoped we could get away with waiting until we got down to 200 metres instead. We thought it would be all right, and our bosses agreed. At 180 metres we stopped to measure the temperature. At first it was rising slowly, but as the gauge approached 180 metres it suddenly rose hotter and hotter. At 180 metres it was more than 200° and still rising. We had reached the critical point.

'To avoid it exploding at any moment we had to put a preventor across, but the thermacouple for measuring the temperature was still in the hole and had to be removed before we could install the preventor. We started to withdraw the thermacouple, knowing this was dangerous, and it was almost out when the first explosion happened with a great roaring and a loud clap, as boiling water and steam erupted, sending a shower of stones into the air. Where they hit the metal of the rig they caused sparks to fly.

'Things were so out of control we had to evacuate the camp. Luckily, there were no casualties. By morning the eruption had finished, leaving a cone of sulphur steam and when we went to investigate we saw a great funnel-shaped hole, ten metres across and five metres deep, with our drill rig and truck destroyed and fallen to the bottom of the hole.'

Another day we went to Gorely, a volcano of several craters and merged cones. We climbed up the lava flow, horrible going on sharp cinders, to a summit which was one of eleven superimposed craters with about thirty vents and lava flows, radial faults, seismic collapses, tectonic deformations and sheets of pumice. Ten years ago it had produced continuous cinder-gas explosions and five years before that it erupted with a million tons of ash. It is due to explode again soon.

The view around the summit was staggering, a string of volcanoes in line to the north, a clear view of Mutnofski and the canyon we had followed into it; and to the north-east we could see the Pacific Ocean.

We picnicked on a side cone of black cinder, then skied down the volcano, traversing on firm fast snow. The continually changing perspectives, and the feeling of being so dwarfed by volcanoes made this one of the most memorable skiing experiences I have had. We never seemed to reach the end, the skis kept running, and every time I thought the slopes had finished, the skis kept going. My only regret was to be on thin bits of plastic and wearing wellies. Wellies indeed! I felt very inept.

'Do you want to drive the vezdehod?' the driver offered. We had said goodbye to the geologists and were on a plateau looking for a river valley called Viluchinski. I had already checked out the controls. They looked simple enough, so I put on the army surplus tank-driver's leather helmet and took over. What a splendid machine. It had just two levers which controlled each track independently, letting me turn sharp corners by stopping one track, or correct course by slowing them in turn.

'Keep your revs higher,' I was warned.

Yes, not a nice place to stall. On the big mountains that flanked the valley the snow had developed sag lines like old women's skin. Spring was on the way. When the going became tricky I gave the controls back to the expert and joined Luda on skis.

We raced each other but she always won. She told me that once in an international relay race a tall opponent had skied alongside her and clamped Luda's head under her arm. She squeezed hard, forcing Luda back, and went into the lead. Luda was so angry it gave her extra strength to overtake the cheat, and Luda's team won the event.

In the valley a hot stream ran past the door of the cabin where we stayed the night. There were dandelions and buttercups, we made nettle soup, and I felt inexplicably content. Next day as we followed Valentin's footprints we saw the paw prints of a large bear superimposed over them. The bear had matched Valentin stride for stride for a couple of kilometres. We lunched ravenously on caviar, wild garlic and

115

bread before exploring the entrance to a gold mine. The tunnel was unsafe, not so much because the wood props were rotten, but because of the poisonous gases that seep into it. The first timber had already fallen but I had brought my torch and went in a little way, water pouring through the roof, until my batteries fizzed and went dim. Valentin said that the temperatures at the deepest part reached 45°.

Mining was but one of the developing industries of Siberia and the Far East. The geologists who came east had already located gold, silver and lignite, and there are grounds for thinking that Kamchatka is rich in both oil and gas. Deposits of iron ore, lead, copper and mercury were being exploited. The mining, metallurgical, chemical and power industries were developing along with agriculture and the fur, timber and fishing industries. What price, I wondered, that National Park.

7

The Land of the Little King

It was Easter when I set off for north-east Kamchatka and the reindeer-breeding region of Achai Vayam where I would spend the next month. To get there I flew to Tilichiki on the coast just north of the neck of the peninsula and drove to Korf. Korf is built on a sand spit between the sea and a river estuary which was still frozen with two metres of ice. But the ocean seldom freezes, because of strong winds in the Bering Sea. When the south wind blows it brings icebergs that stack up in the bay. The sand under the town is continually being eroded and two main streets have long since been washed away. Waves frequently flood over the sand spit leaving people's houses knee-deep in seawater.

I would spend the Easter holiday in Korf, waiting for the twice-weekly helicopter to Achai Vayam. Valentin and Natasha were still with me, it was the first time either of them had been this far north. We stayed with a geologist called Leonid and his wife Tanya, and I shared a bedroom with a mass of seedlings due to be planted out in the greenhouse. My bedside table was covered in young tomatoes, radishes, cucumbers, and courgettes. Only the potatoes live out, the ground being sandy, so it doesn't freeze too much.

Every surface in the living-room was decorated with Leonid's collection of stones and slices of rock, polished agates and amethyst, fossilised wood and coral, petrified cross-sections of undersea worm casts, and a fossilised oyster with a fossilised pearl in it. There was vivid blue lazerite, charoit of vibrant purple, the only known deposit of which in the world is in Siberia, and Leonid showed me flowery brown jasper, black and red striped jaspilit, limonit, and whorls of red mercury in yellow sulphur. Pecalit is like threads of silky cream rock, here threaded with grey zinc. To cut the rock Leonid uses an old diamond-cutting blade and two flat polishing wheels, one covered in leather that you wet with water, the other of metal you put wet diamond dust on and polish for an hour.

My first evening we joined a group of Leonid's colleagues to start celebrating Easter. Valentin warned me off the geologists' vodka. It smelt like nail-polish remover. They say the home-made stuff is similar to the fuel that sends rockets to the moon. Early on Easter Sunday morning I went with Tanya to collect eggs from her chickens to dye in different colours for breakfast. Then a neighbour came over, the first of several visitors, bringing a tall thin cake. Tanya had also baked some of the same unusual shape. I asked if they use a special Easter cake tin and she said yes, pointing to the tin mugs everyone drinks tea from.

Late morning we set off for a barbecue on the beach of black sand covered in great thick slabs of ice. The sea was full of big chunks of ice, too, which rocked in the surf, jostling and bumping like mini icebergs – ice on sea, sea on ice, ice on ice, black-backed gulls wheeling and diving for fish. Out beyond the ice was clear ocean where an occasional seal poked its head up to look around. I wandered along looking for whale bones. Natasha was looking for precious stones and found two pieces of jasper.

The barbecue took place beyond the fish factory among some half-derelict fishing boats, where we found a piece of decking to use as a table on which to spread our Easter feast: shish kebabs of mutton, roasted bits of chicken, spring onions, bowls of buckwheat, and assorted tall thin cakes whose icing melted when snow began falling. We had plenty of home-made vodka to keep our spirits up in the cold snow. Someone poured me some green 'vodka' and Valentin, ever mindful of my survival, told me not to touch it.

There was a strange mood at the party with people voicing their fears about their jobs, as it seemed likely the geology units would be closed down, and they did not know what the future held. I noticed how people blamed the state, there was no sense of personal responsibility for life. They were the chattels of the state, the state had always looked after them and made the conditions of life for them. They could see no possibility of looking for work elsewhere, there were no private companies, no employer but the state. They did not see why they should leave or look for more menial work.

Valentin said the system had made people lazy. They were paid for work regardless of its standard; there was no incentive, no pride in work. I tried to explain that if you lose your job you should look for a new job and go to evening classes for extra qualifications. The Russians said why should they, it was the state's problem not theirs.

Two days later we flew over a large marshy basin, and hundreds of small lakes, to land eventually at the remote settlement of Achai Vayam.

We were met by the Director of the state farm, a small rotund man named Yeprintsev, and by the Chukchi lady Governor, Claudia, who installed us in the house formerly reserved for visiting Communist Party bosses. It was large by Russian standards, having a lobby, three bedrooms, kitchen and bathroom. If wealth is judged by the carpets hung on walls, someone here was trying to impress their bosses, as every room had at least two wall-carpets, but very saggy spring beds, from the days when those Communist bosses grew fat. In this season Achai Vayam was a marsh, and you needed rubber boots to walk along the only street, boasting a shop, a club, a little hospital, and small wooden houses. The inhabitants were Chukchi, Eveni and a few Russians.

Scattered around the outskirts were the *yurangas* of Chukchi families. Unlike the square tents of Koryak deer camps, these are round and large, about eight metres across. We waded out to one belonging to Claudia's family, stamping our feet energetically outside not just to clean off the mud and snow, but to tell the occupants they had visitors – a stamper instead of a knocker. Dogs howled in response and an old woman with tattooed face came out. Her tattoos were two hour-glass lines from top of forehead to end of nose, and her dress was of traditional Chukchi skins.

Claudia introduced us and ushered us inside, which was spacious, with chests, sleds, and boxes around the perimeter, and a large sleeping-area called a *polok*, curtained with hanging deerskins on all sides, the front tied open during the day.

Standing by it was the Chukchi head of the family, an old man born around 1906, on crutches now and very deaf, but his mind was bright. His name was Aimek which means spicy. Aimek had been the wealthy owner of three thousand deer before collectivisation by the state farm had stripped him of his life savings. He has been poor since Communism began.

Dogs barked again and feet stamped as their daughter Nuteney (meaning tundra) arrived. She had a more intricate pattern of tattoos on her face but told us tattooing was a matter of personal whim, it had no clan significance, though it once used to indicate a wealthy family. To make the marks women use a needle and match-heads.

Chukchi are different from Koryak people in customs and language. Their homeland, Chukotsk, is the peninsula facing the Bering Strait, a few hundred kilometres north of us. Reindeer Koryak used to be proud and rich, treating the poorer maritime Koryak as their slaves. But when meeting the Chukchi, even the reindeer Koryak were humble. The Chukchi used to have a reputation for being devious and cunning, and I had read that they were overbearing, inhospitable, thieving, their whole object in life to put one over someone else by trickery.

Keener fighters than either the Koryak or Eskimo, they were never conquered by the Russians, they forced them to a treaty. As with the Koryaks, there are maritime and reindeer Chukchi, with different beliefs according to the animals they live by.

We visited other yurangas, some rather smoky, as the hole at the top is also the meeting point for the mass of poles which hold up these big tents. The sides are supported by curved frame poles and the top is held up by a four-metre pole and a big tripod with the fireplace below. Pussywillow twigs to celebrate the birth of the reindeer calves decorated the hearth and native butter was being skimmed off a cauldron of bones to anoint the totems or *gitchgee* which reminded me of those I had seen in the north-west. Those were kept together in one hut, but here they were in evidence in every yuranga and in frequent use. I tried to find out more about them.

The biggest totems were simplistic and human shaped. They are carved at the time of marriage and the creation of a home, as you cannot possess a protector until you have your own yuranga to protect. Wooden forked pegs, *oka-mak*, represent reindeer, and are hung in the yuranga entrance if deer are lost or wandering. Tiny sacks of deerskin with fur inside are protection from misfortune and are usually made if one of the family has a dream with bad omens. For example, to dream of a fox, means bad luck is coming. Small gitchgee carvings can be helpers for the larger totems.

Hanging separately was a pipe smoked at certain celebrations, decorated with beads and pouches, and inherited paternally. The quantity of totems depends on the number of sons in a family. The main protectors are inherited by the youngest son, who will also inherit the yuranga, not the eldest.

We made our way back through the swamp of tussocks with red mosses and water everywhere; fortunately I was wearing my Palana waders. Valentin wasn't and he got soaked to the knees, while he and Natasha bickered. They were determined to find fault with each other. Not that Valentin had really got along with anyone we met: he hated Boris the vulcanologist and Vitali the bear man; he probably disliked us all. But I liked him and tried to look after him because, despite his huge size, he was somehow vulnerable.

After a banyo with the Director's wife we had supper at their house and Director Yeprintsev told us about the administration of ten thousand reindeer. Yeprintsev is what you might call a little king, ruling over two million hectares of land, and about eight hundred subjects, not to mention the deer. He is king because no one dares to refuse him anything; he controls earnings and food supplies. The royal livestock includes horses, milk cattle, chickens; and he employs ten professional hunters to supply skins and fur and, when not hunting, they work at fishing and caviar harvesting. Dinner was excellent, and the Little King promised to provide us with transport to see the region.

There would be a royal performance of song and dance by Chukchi and Eveni the following evening, so in the morning I asked Claudia to introduce us to an Even family. They consider themselves more sophisticated than Chukchi, from whom they differ in lots of ways like the construction of tents or snowshoes. But one of the main differences is that the Eveni are Christian, and where the Chukchi surround themselves with hut totems, the Eveni have carved wooden icons which are kept in the east corner of the house or yuranga. One woman told me she stands in front of the icon to pray every morning and evening. The only church in Kamchatka is in Petropavlovsk.

Older practices linger on, however. After death the Chukchi have cremations and sacrifice deer at Shaman Mountain, the Eveni bury their dead but sacrifice deer at the cemetery after making the sign of the cross. Their Christian crosses are decorated with pairs of antlers.

Claudia introduced me to a delightful young Even woman, Victoria, who showed me her family icon, given to her by her mother, and to her mother by hers. It was presented to her grandmother when she married. The icon was twenty-five centimetres by fifteen, Christ on a Russian Orthodox cross with a wonderful lustre from generations of being handled and stroked. Victoria was one of the dancers we watched that evening doing a reindeer dance which imitated the beast pawing the ground to seek moss under the snow. She and three other young women also sang, standing in a tight square, and made deer huffing noises. Unlike the Koryaks who dance crouched forward, the Eveni are more upright, even the bottom-waggling routine is more upright. It's called *pohacha*, which translates as arse-dancing.

From art to reality, the next day we set off for a month to visit some reindeer-breeding camps about 120 kilometres away, accompanied by Yeprintsev. The Little King had rustled up the latest thing in transport, an environmentally friendly vezdehod of the latest design. Its driver, Vladimir, said only a hundred of this type had been made. Their lighter more open construction means they churn up less of the tundra but, unlike the old amphibious vezdehods, they cannot swim. However, they're tall enough to drive through quite deep rivers and, after leaning out nervously to assess the first couple we crossed, I just trusted to Vladimir.

Certainly the activity seemed to allow for an unusual degree of trial and error. Driving up a long low cliff, the engine failed to get us to the top at one wet muddy place and, when it stalled, we ran backwards down a seventy-degree slope. No one fussed, I guessed it was normal. When we came to a halt Vladimir simply refired the engine and in lowest gear we clawed our way up in a smokescreen of black exhaust.

In fact Vladimir was one of the most experienced vezdehod drivers in the territory and, unwilling to depend on local guides as previous drivers had done, he had set himself to learn about the terrain, and in particular to find the safest river crossings. He was very much liked by the far-flung communities to whom he brought supplies, and valued as a calm and practical hero of many rescue dashes.

Now we clanked on at ten k.p.h. across eternal tundra – nothingness, except for odd colours of pale lichen, and red weed, like the Martian attack in *War of the Worlds*. Bits of space were filled with skeletal trees, contorted and stunted by the weather. We could see where some deer-herdsmen had camped. They left an arrow at the site to show which direction they had gone. The blizzard, which had accompanied us most of the morning, slackened again and we saw the blur of distant knuckles on rock fingers, that were the Glove Mountains. The land became hilly with marshy bowls and peat bogs. We thumped and jolted over tussocks, into a district of small lakes in bowls, more emptiness, and beautiful moorland where moose went cantering away from us.

The Little King was asleep on a pile of deerskins in his khaki dungarees and Chukchi two-cornered fur hat framing his round face which, with his two gold teeth and brown beard, made him look like a gnome.

We reached the first herders' camp, or *tabun*, by late afternoon and shared some fish we had freshly caught along the way with the brigade of eight men and women. The fish were succulent, and they produced a haunch of last year's deer meat which had been left out all winter in airtight wrapping. It was not so tender but still very edible. I was offered a delicacy, the end of the reindeer's tongue, and was surprised when what I was given was already missing its tip. The reason for this was explained by the Chukchi Number Two of the state farm, a man called Yvtagin. 'It is traditional because animals used to talk too much. Reindeer and dogs in particular. Dogs usually made rude remarks about the disgusting things humans do. And reindeer loved to complain. So the Supreme Being cut off the tip of the dog's tongue, which is why dogs can no longer speak, and people cut off the tip of the reindeer's tongue to stop it complaining.'

At seven p.m. we piled back into the vezdehod. Flat-topped mountains appeared to both sides and at a dry riverbed we paused to gather firewood and tent poles which we would need later, since we were clearly going to be camping out that night. I looked for fossilised wood which Vladimir said could be found there, but saw only the footprints of bears and moose. At the next river-crossing there was a great crack in the ice and I put on my fur hat to act as a crash helmet. We started across, and there was a loud groan as the ice split and pale green and turquoise water appeared. My fellow passengers did gasp this time. But we only fell a short way and the vezdehod managed to pull itself out of the water.

The surroundings grew more grandiose, steeper volcanic hills with giant basalt plugs, eroded into pillars. Our valley became too narrow for the vezdehod to keep to the banks so we drove along the riverbed towards a cluster of plug-topped hills. Grinding over rock spills and around headlands, we finally came to a gorgeous spot by a lake and stopped to make camp.

Our party consisted of the Little King, Yvtagin, two other Chukchi, Vladimir, Natasha, Valentin and myself. We would all share one tent with a fire inside and a tin chimney. For a bed we cut a mattress of cedar branches to keep us off the wet ground, and laid deerskins and sleeping-bags on top. And since the night would be cold we slept in *chaji* fur socks, as well as all our clothes and hats.

Not too early we woke, breakfasted on salmon caviar and, packing the tent, drove north into a new valley, running like a great avenue between shark's-tooth mountains, huge natural pyramids like soldiers in line guarding a pass, which we crossed to enter a splendid mountainous region. A snow ram with its great corkscrew horns went leaping up a gulley ahead of us in big bounds.

At an abandoned tabun we stopped to collect a deerskin tent. Now was the time of changeover between winter and spring, and skin tents were being stored in favour of canvas tents for the summer. The odd thing about this area was its almost complete lack of snow.

We reached an inhabited tabun, where a stillborn deerskin was hung on a pole to dry. The herdsmen separate the males and females about two weeks before calving, as the pace of the males becomes too much for the females. Taking four herdsmen for a change of duty, we drove on upriver to see the furthest tabun, ten kilometres away on the border between Kamchatka and Chukotka, which is marked by a huge permanently glaciated mountain. It was a stunning place of peaks soaring into wispy cloud, and the headwaters of the Apuca river, a snowmelt area with multiple glacier valleys. The herdsmens' dogs ran alongside the vezdehod. At streams they swam, or the clever ones leaped from ice-floe to ice-floe, and when they spotted a white Arctic hare, they all gave chase in a new burst of speed.

I wanted to see the female herd and their new calves, called *cai-yu-yu*, so while the vezdehod went on to the male herd with two changeover men, the rest of us followed Yvtagin as stealthily as possible so as not to alarm the reindeer, and risk stampeding them with their calves. He whistled softly when we passed near a group of a hundred, fat with pregnancy; deer waiting to calve tend to congregate naturally together, and go off alone when ready to give birth. We climbed on to where nearly a thousand deer and their young were grazing. The oldest cai-yu-yu were three weeks old, most were only a week, and I watched a white one, born the day before, dancing over to his mother for milk. By some bushes a doe was licking her newborn bundle. It rose, wobbled, pranced, fell, then stood puzzled trying to work out how to use legs. An extraordinary instinct takes it from birth into full active life.

We scrambled up to a high point overlooking the herd where the duty shepherds had made a small fire for tea, as the Little King had brought new supplies of sugar and bread. The sun sank slowly while we sat watching the antics of the young deer.

For the herdsmen this season called *Kitkitki* in early spring is one of the busiest times of year, when they divide the herd, oversee the birth of young, then attend to the gelding of non-breeding stock males.

Late spring is *Kitti-ga*, when deer stop eating moss and lichen and go for the first green shoots of grass on riverbanks. Snow is melting, and it is time to start training race deer.

Early summer, *An-nok*, is when the first leaves appear. The herd scatters easily as they forage. This is the season to slaughter for drying meat, and the women collect deer droppings for curing deerskins. It ends when the first warble flies lay eggs in the deer's belly skin.

Kalatinga is mid-summer, a time to keep the herd moving towards the coast, away from the flies. The deer want to face into the wind to get rid of the flies, which is inconvenient if the herdsmen want them to go in another direction. An extra problem in summer is when hooves begin to crack from the constant change of wet to dry, and the deer grow nervous as the mosquitoes breed, scattering easily.

Letofka is the time when the herd reaches the coast and drinks seawater. This is important for its fattening minerals. The herdsmen make sure the animals arrive thirsty, then spend a few dry days inland before having another dose of saltwater.

Khan-rak-tat, autumn, is difficult since, given a chance, the deer eat the many magic mushrooms then in season which make them excitable and disobedient. The deep winter is less arduous because there is little to do but look after and protect the herd from bears and beasts of prey, and to train new deer for pulling sleds.

I watched the men's lean, healthy faces as we talked, their sharp eyes calmly checking the flock. It seemed a world away from the drunken herdsmen I had met seven weeks ago near Lesnoe who had lost their herd.

At sunset we made our way down and back to the tabun. A deer which had broken its leg was being butchered by the two women. They worked swiftly, throwing a line of pieces on the blood-splattered snow: heart, liver, penis (for medicinal purposes), joints, and ribs which they chopped with an axe.

Their children took slivers of glass and started slicing open the bubbled maggot cases in the deerskin to squeeze out a fat white grub the size of my fingernail. Yvtagin explained they eat them like sweets but these were not yet ripe. They would have to wait a couple of weeks until the grubs turned black. I was promised a different delicacy for supper, the soft pantui on the young deer antlers.

A little girl of three was dreamily poking her fingers round the eyeball sockets of the dead deer. Oxana had had her name changed three times so far. The first name was given by her grandmother because it was the name of the ancestor whose soul was thought to be in the child, but she fell ill and a divining stone was used to discover her real soul. The close family gathered and while the stone swung from its tripod, they called out names of dead relatives. When the right name was called the stone turned faster on its thread. Another simpler way of determining whose soul is in the child is by calling out names and judging from the infant's reaction to them. Cries denote the wrong names, smiles for the correct one. Souls of newborn children come from the top world of the Supreme Being, where they hang on straps from the rafters and crossbeams of his house until the time comes for them to be reborn.

This little girl was renamed Ankak. Again the soul didn't fit and she became ill. The third time her name was changed to Oxana, who now looked perfectly healthy and something of a handful. At supper she used a hunting knife like her elders to cut the meat from her mouth, then played with the matches, trying to set fire to the woodpile.

Names can be changed at any age, even in mid-life, and Yvtagin said his was changed when he was thirty-five, since he broke the same leg twice and it wouldn't heal for a year. Then an aunt had a dream and remembered an ancestor who had a bad open leg-break, and suggested he take that man's name. So he did, and quite soon his leg mended naturally and strongly, and has given him no trouble since then.

He said the key is to fit the relative to the illness. When Claudia's baby son went blind and began bleeding from his navel, the family remembered a blind great-grandfather but could not recall his name. The infant grew weaker, then one night in a dream Claudia was told the ancestor's name. Her son was renamed and his eyes recovered.

On our way to visit the third tabun the Little King wanted to speak to his subjects and tell them we were coming, so we attached the radio crank handle to the side of the vezdehod, and tossed an empty bottle with a line attached up to the top branches of a birch tree as an antenna. Though the Chukchi cranked like mad he could not make the radio work. En route once more, we spotted three lynx, big cats with tawny fur and ear tufts, so stopped for a royal hunt. Yeprintsev and three men took the dog and went tracking across the snow. Rather than get shot by mistake I stayed on the vezdehod as it crossed a river, cracking up in the early thaw. We tipped over sharply in a deep pool, but clung to the sides and the machine eventually hauled itself out. The only person to roll a vez-dehod completely, I was told, was the Little King who some years ago drove into a gulley, tipping some of his passengers out and almost rolled over them. After one futile shot at the lynx, the hunting party returned and we went on our journey.

'Do you want a go at driving a pair of race reindeer?' I was asked.

Reindeer racing is a traditional sport which has existed here since pre-history. At the tabun we visited that day I was given a chance to try my hand. The first thing you have to re-member is that deer are handled only from the right side, never from the left, and I quickly learned that if you ever approach or walk on their left they are afraid. This makes har-nessing a pair a mite complicated for a beginner and involves a lot of putting your arm around the right-hand deer's neck and leaning over it with loops and straps in a thoroughly over-familiar way. Lastly, you put each thumb through a loop at the end of the reins, wrap them twice backwards around your mittens and, the moment you sit down, off you go.

I started by tooling around on the grass since the springtime runners are designed to go on snow or wet grass. The undersides are covered traditionally with baleen, the part of the whale's throat that separates water and plankton and was known to the Western world for its use in women's corsets. But plastic is now creeping in, even in Kamchatka. The sled is meant to run on the right of the deer's hindlegs, and my major difficulty was left turns, since the left rein went between the deer and didn't produce results unless I also flapped the right rein.

The deer seemed obedient and worked hard to pull over tussocks and low birch bushes. To go faster I had been given a long springy whip tipped with a walrus tooth, but it was not necessary to use it and we sped along. Unlike a horse's trot which has diagonal steps, deer trot with parallel legs, and sometimes all four feet seem to be in the air at once. After we hit one cedar clump at speed and a branch got tangled in the harness, I looked for somewhere snowy and headed for a distant lake.

All around the edge the ice was firm and at first things went well, steering at a smart trot, going up the bank and back down to the ice. But the extra speed excited the deer, and they began to jump around. I put down my heels, useless as brakes on the ice, and I feared the noise was alarming the deer but the sled was still going and I succeeded in doing a figure-of-eight while looking for a good stretch of firm ice. Then things went wrong.

The deer's hooves were slipping and they panicked. I put my feet down to brake but they went crazy. Their hooves shot in every direction. The sled went out of control and the reindeer bolted. It seemed a long nightmare on ice until I steered them off into snow and bushes, deer's legs plunging, my feet still down trying to slow the sled. My boot suddenly caught in a bush, I flew in the air, there was a sharp pain in my ankle, but I still had the reins in my hands. I landed near the sled and got dragged at a gallop, over ice again and light snow. Finally they stopped. I felt a bit sick with shock.

I was shaking all over and the deer were still in a wild mood; I couldn't stand so had to get back on the sled and collect my nerves. My clothes were soaked and my foot felt numb. As I drove back over the grassy tundra I realised I had been mad to drive on the ice. Of course it would be slippery, I just hadn't thought it through. With luck my foot was only sprained. It didn't feel like a broken ankle.

The camp was being packed up to move to fresh pasture when I got back. I managed to get my boot off, and knew I wouldn't be able to put it on again for several days, the foot was swelling rapidly. Everything was loaded into the vezdehod, including sleds and dogs which we dropped off an hour later, and we all settled down like sardines. The King heaped deerskins on us for warmth.

Beside me Yvtagin was sympathetic to my blunder and told me the terrible trouble he had had with ice when he first began deer-sledding. His nightmare didn't stop until the deer's legs tangled in the reins, and as he tried to untangle them one deer swung its horns violently sideways, butting him to the ground and trampling him. Terrified he rolled away, far too afraid to drive the deer home. The next time he was given the same deer to drive he kept the reins short.

On my other side was Valentin who said Yvtagin was rather like a reindeer himself; every few minutes while they were walking Yvtagin had been making funny huffing noises. Valentin had offered to carry his knapsack but Yvtagin said, No, no, the noises were just a habit.

I was buried under eight skins and furs, so heavy I couldn't move, though I finally freed my nose from its covers and watched the stars. Vladimir occasionally turned on his one remaining headlight to check the path. Some girls from the tabun we were giving a lift to said you sometimes saw distant fires at night but as the vezdehod approached there was nothing there. Their elders had told them these were their ancestors warning the young not to forget the dead, and reminding them they must make a sacrifice, maybe only a small thing, like a piece of chocolate or a cigarette. Hours jolted past, and the galaxies moved imperceptibly. The Little King stood the whole time, upright behind the driver's cab, to help find the way, and I dozed to the slushing sound of wet snow, rattling of boulders, roaring of the motor and grinding of gears. We reached Achai Vayam at two-thirty a.m.

The next morning I couldn't walk, so asked Natasha and Valentin to find me a pair of crutches and some form of transport. My two helpers were giving trouble. They had started squabbling with increasing venom. Valentin called Natasha, 'Hey you fish without brains,' and they began arguing again at breakfast about a scented twig I had picked and asked them to identify. Valentin said rhododendron, Natasha insisted juniper, and they were betting their clothes on the result. Valentin tried on Natasha's trousers saying he would win. They came back with crutches for me but of a height to fit Chukchi people, so that I had to stoop over to use them. But they were better than nothing and I soon got the hang of them and went off to visit Yvtagin's family yuranga where we had been invited to eat pantui and celebrate *Kil-vay*, the reindeer calving, one of the most important festivals of the Chukchi year.

The head of Yvtagin's family was a matriarch called Tungan, which means Blossoming.

'Deer are the source of life,' she told me.

Some tall sprigs of pussywillow were brought in and set to stretch upwards, symbolising the spring of new life. Guests arrived and wished each other good fortune. Tungan showed me how yesterday she had marked certain people's faces on both cheeks with blood. Mine she now marked just with her index finger. The food for the feast was breast of reindeer, boiled with young grasses, berries and seal fat. Offerings of meat were put out for nature's diverse elements, for the sky, sun, moon, water and willow trees.

Just as winter tents were giving way to summer ones, so skins were being abandoned in favour of the spring-summer garb of khaki smocks over baggy khaki trousers for men, and cotton smocks for women, coming just below the knee, and decorated with red and pink bands round hems, cuffs and sleeves.

The pantui was singed on the fire for five minutes before it was ready for scraping and eating. It tasted quite sweet, not like meat, and had a thick skin-like soft cartilege. Then you suck the inner bone to draw sweet blood. I asked about pantui's medicinal properties and learned it alleviates stress and is given to convalescents.

'But if you eat too much you may fall asleep,' Tungan warned.

Natasha, Valentin and I joined the family around the hearth to singe the pantui. Nobody is allowed to cross the fire-place, even if there is no fire in it. The hearth was ringed with stones, and when I asked what was the oldest thing in the yuranga Tungan pointed to two hearth stones polished with butter, one sitting in a deerskin pouch. 'Those came many hundreds of years ago, they are sacred to the fire. Men inherit family stones when they marry and build their first yuranga.'

Next she smeared fat on the protecting totems, murmuring words of ritual affection to them as she rubbed the butter in. 'If I leave out even one, it will be offended.' The protectors were then put on a sled and taken out into the daylight. They would be left outside until the next morning, since the baby deer festival continued over several days.

At this time the women pray that the calves may be numerous, strong, grow quickly, and find enough food. The ritual words are passed from generation to generation, taught by mothers to daughters. For this ceremony butter-fat is mixed with snow, which makes it turn very white.

I noticed a large skull just inside the sleeping area, prob-ably a bear skull. Yvtagin saw my glance and said, 'Please don't ask me about that, it is taboo. We have already shared many secrets with you.' I respected his wishes. It was un-doubtedly a protector, for Chukchi believe bears keep away evil spirits, and some say a bear's skull protects one from werewolves.

Yvtagin's son turned up to give us a lift home on his motor-bike. I sat in the sidecar with my foot sticking out, while Natasha rode pillion and Valentin perched on the wheel arch. Their quarrel was unresolved since we had lost the twig to be identified, but a new dispute had arisen about the role of women. Valentin, an old-fashioned boy, was furious because Natasha was a useless cook and didn't know how to keep house. He accused her of being vain and lazy, their characters just seemed to collide. Natasha described herself as a Leo, being like a cat, kind yet angry, mild yet fierce, and needing to be admired. Vain, yes so be it. Her admirers already included Vladimir and the Little King, whose wife was beginning to bristle with jealousy now we were home.

Late in the afternoon Valentin woke up from his overdose of pantui and we had a huge treat because, despite her anger, the Queen baked some cakes and she sent us one with blue-berry and chocolate icing. We demolished half the cake in minutes, then Valentin made a comment about Natasha being fat, the quarrel reactivated and I covered the cake as if they were children, refusing them more until they promised to behave.

Vladimir, the vezdehod driver, and his family invited us for supper, and we persuaded him to talk more about the perils of his work. Once he startled a bear which ran parallel to the vezdehod, so Vladimir decided to see which could go faster. The bear reached forty k.p.h., and the vezdehod kept pace. I bet that was when he broke all the shock absorbers. When they reached the trees, the vezdehod had to stop, but the bear didn't slow down and Vladimir was impressed by the way the trees shook as it fled.

A herder Vladimir once rescued had not been so lucky when he disturbed a mother bear protecting cubs. Vladimir described how the man was scalped and his body so badly mauled his lungs were visible. He was in shock when Vladimir arrived to the rescue, bringing a vet, vodka and Golden Root.

Claudia's aunt, Nayun, said she had to sacrifice one of her dogs, the old white one, for although none of her family was ill at that moment, she wanted to protect her grandchildren by this gesture. As gestures go it was a considerable one for the Chukchi are kind to their dogs, believing that they protect them against the kalau. The gates to the Upper World are also guarded by dogs, and if you have been cruel to dogs in your lifetime they will be avenged by biting you or refusing you entry, so you will die for ever.

I noticed the protector totems were on display and was given permission to handle them. In a skin bag I found a reindeer kneebone.

'Oh, so that's where we put it,' Nayun said, pleased, 'It's part of the sacred implements we use in fire-making. It's the handle. You put the drill-stick between the kneebone and the dent in this totem's stomach.' I was surprised it fitted so neatly into the belly button in the male figure. 'To make it spark we use this bow of deer antler and leather thong, looped round the drill-stick to spin it into a tinder of dry moss. One person moves the bow, one holds the totem and another the handle; the drill spins like this.' She and her family demonstrated. 'This one is *Mel-gir-gir*, it's used for fire-making at calving and slaughter time.'

Fire-lighting is kept in the family. You can only kindle a fire with embers from the yuranga of your father, sons or grandsons. Giving fire to someone means you give your health and life force. The same goes for idols, pots and many domestic items.

The dog which was due to be sacrificed was brought into the yuranga on a rope, an old laika, retired from its deer-herding days. Nayun said, 'Sometimes we kill the dog with knives. Today it will be killed by a spear. Usually we sacrifice two or three dogs a year, to remember the dead, to celebrate the slaughter season and, like today, as a request to keep our children healthy.'

The family was gathering, three sons and seven grand-children. Nayun's fourth son came in carrying his spear. But they had to wait for all the family to be present before the dog's head would be cut off and put on a pole outside the yuranga. If sacrificed for the dead, the dog's head would point west, and for life, the head points east. The body would be split down the backbone then cut in traverse slashes, and left outside for the ravens to eat. Natasha stopped translating pro-perly at that point, complaining it was all too revolting.

Unlike the Koryak, the Chukchi do not revere the raven as a god but as a mediator between the Lower and Upper worlds. It foretells death when it calls '*collo-collo*,' meaning 'next, next'. Yvtagin said yesterday a raven collo-ed at him and he had shouted back, 'Let you be next.' Ravens also guide a dying man's soul to the Upper World, for which reason they are never killed.

Feeding the dead dog to the ravens would be their way of making sure their prayer reached its destination. The rest of the family had not yet arrived and, as we had a date with the Little King, we left before the dog met its appointed end.

At dinner with Director Yeprintsev I began to piece to-gether his story; he was expelled from school, didn't care about schoolwork, and his father died while he was very young. To that point his story resembled that of various other Kamchatka Russians. His mother was leader of the tractor bri-gade at an agricultural unit in the Crimea. He and his brother and sister also worked at the unit. Maybe that hard menial labour was the start of his self-discipline. For his military ser-vice he did three years in submarines; I pictured him in the conning tower of his vezdehod. After a year as an officer he returned to civilian life and decided to try to qualify at a tech-nical institute, but he was expelled for alcoholism. Next he entered a veterinary college and six years later qualified with honours.

The following day there was further trouble arising from Natasha's ongoing flirtation with Yeprintsev and she realised she must put an end to it. So when we saw him out walking with his wife, Natasha pulled Valentin's arm round her and smiled lovingly up at him. They agreed to pretend to be in love, and I wondered what trouble that would cause. It certainly calmed down the Queen but the Little King became jealous instead. My helpful suggestion that Valentin should stir up the situation by flirting outrageously with the Queen was not well received.

Another evening we had supper with Yvtagin, fish soup using teaspoons to drink from. Yvtagin apologised for not having any normal-sized spoons because he had made them into fishing lures.

Claudia came over with an invitation from her mother-in-law, Koyan (deer). We walked there through big snowflakes, as each day I was determined to use my foot more, and arrived at a scene of much domestic activity and good-natured grumbling. Koyan was at the store tent hanging strips of meat out to dry, and muttering that the weather was too damp for it, while her neighbour was up a ladder scraping snow off the yuranga roof with a right-angled shovel made from a bear's shoulderblade. Her brother who was twisting a new rope for his fishing net was saying, 'What's the point in trying to put fish out for drying while you're still pulling snow off the roof?' Which seemed the sort of remark brothers make the world over.

We sat by the wood stove to talk and listen to Koyan who was born long before the Russians came to Kamchatka in the 1930s. She remembered how afraid she had been of their horses and their aeroplanes. The Chukchi people thought planes must be witches that lived beyond the sunset, and they protected themselves against such magic by mixing deer intestine-fat with hare's fur and smearing it on birch bark

137

positioned to face the setting sun. It may have protected them from harm by planes, but not against the Russians who collectivised them.

Koyan had been a herder, working for her father. She liked her work in the tundra, and in time she fell in love with a young man. Her father refused to allow the marriage and instead married her off to a rich old man. Her tabun and the young man's were in frequent contact, and she could never forget him. The love she felt was like being weightless, she said. Their affair was limited to their eyes which seemed to touch each other's souls. And he would sing her song.

Every Chukchi has his or her own song which is a tune they make up in their own minds and only share with a would-be lover as a way of declaring love. Then Koyan sang me her song, a deep slow melody. After the first verse her voice suddenly caught alight, ringing out strongly, but it still gave her pain to sing of love, and her voice began fading away until it was just a whisper.

As for Claudia, she had taken a long time before she grew her own song, then one day it came to her. She had two special admirers. One was Koyan's son Anatoly and the other, not surprising perhaps, was our friend Yvtagin. By chance both men sent offers of marriage to her on the same day. Yvtagin was coming from one direction by deer-sled, having received his parents' blessing to the idea, and Anatoly's relatives were bringing his offer from the opposite direction. The latter arrived in the morning, and the offer was accepted at noon. Yvtagin arrived in the evening, simply too late.

'But we're all happy now and things mostly happen in a way that's best for all,' said Claudia contentedly. A reindeer is usually sacrificed at a marriage, killed as always from the left side, which is partly why deer fear approach from that side. The sacrificial deer foretells your happiness. If it dies calmly the marriage will be strong, if it lashes in agony it will be painful, and if the dying deer struggles to a new place, the wife will not stay long. Claudia's deer had died quietly.

Other sacrifices are made to the points of sunrise and sunset, and blood is daubed on the faces of bride and groom. This part of the ceremony is called *Alarantu urgin*, the journey out of loneliness. Claudia smeared blood on the sleds, and on the totems, and finally on the fireplace where she said the ritual words '*Mimeleu hatvarkim*' (may all be well).

No bride price is paid, but presents are given and everyone takes part in the feast. Claudia has her own bunch of reindeer, which remain hers, even if she leaves her husband. When the family needs meat her husband kills one of his deer, for to slaughter hers would imply he could not provide for his family.

Traditional Chukchi marriages are now a thing of the past, as is the custom of the bridegroom working as a servant for his future father-in-law for months or sometimes years and having to undergo severe tests. Claudia's husband had served for her by going hunting and fishing for her father.

If a wife leaves her husband she may not take her children, they belong paternally. Early marriages are considered bad for a girl's health and if a very young Chukchi girl bears a child she is called a 'fawn mother'. In the Chukchi language there is no word for 'girl', and virginity is not required or expected. Bur rape is a serious crime, and despite the former habit of exchanging partners with visiting guests, the Chukchi are not promiscuous. On the contrary, they seemed more moral than the Russians.

Some of the King's horses and one of his men turned up to offer me an afternoon's adventure. I hoped Valentin wouldn't be the Humpty Dumpty, as he mounted from the wrong side but he assured me he could ride a horse. He said he had spent two months on horseback geologising in Siberia. He didn't say until afterwards that the horses were so old they never went faster than a shuffling walk.

So Valentin, a Chukchi lad called Cuola and I set off. My steed was very shaggy, fast, and easy to ride. I pushed it into a canter and began to enjoy the ride. A muddy track led us to the tea-coloured Achai Vayam river, the melted part now in spate with great chunks of ice moving downstream. As we watched, a massive piece snagged and caused a crunching pile-up of mini-icebergs until the dam broke.

We tracked alongside another river and came to the back of Shaman Mountain where it falls in cliffs. Forging our way through snowdrifts and bushes, I pulled my knees up to the pony's withers, there wasn't an inch to spare. After circling the base of the hills we turned back towards Achai Vayam and Valentin's steed broke into a gallop. I doubted he would be able to stop, so I let mine gallop, too, and we all pounded along. I caught sight of Cuolo's huge smile, and when I over-took Valentin I saw his face alight with exhilaration.

Another day Claudia took us for a close look at Shaman Mountain, two kilometres from the settlement, where Chuk-chi cremations still take place. It has a flattened top and many levelled patches where pyres have blazed and funeral sports of wrestling, ball games, even card-playing take place.

The pyre is of cedar wood, and the body is placed on it wearing special funeral clothes sewn with untidy stitches so that in the Upper World the clothes will be made perfect. The women remove grasses that have protected the dead person's mouth against kalau, and caw like ravens, asking the birds to take the soul to heaven. A special piece of wood is prepared for fire-lighting and passed around the family circle, each of whom in turn adds flames to the pyre. Every bit of open ground was covered in charred wood, and channels had been dug, to prevent the fires spreading.

Reindeer sacrifice is, as one might expect, an important part of the ceremonial. Claudia said her husband's father, born in 1902, keeps saying he is ready to die, so every year Claudia has to prepare two reindeer to sacrifice for him. He hadn't died, but Claudia still had to sacrifice the reindeer and bring two more up to standard. They must be racing deer, which are sacrificed at the point when they are ready to race.

Various spots were marked by heaps of reindeer bones. Claudia said there should be stacks of antlers too, but they had been gathered and sold at the instigation of the Little King. For fifteen dollars a kilo their ancestors had been exposed to sacrilege.

We wandered over the mountain, boggy and ideal for holding back fires, coming upon oddments like a bowl, a knife, a jar, forgotten things the dead were meant to take with them on the journey ahead. Women are given sewing things, men knives, both are given tea and food for the road. All sacrificed animals are believed to join large heavenly herds belonging to the dead. Though most Chukchi believe in a simple Upper World above ours, and that people who die in one world are reborn in the other, there is apparently also a system of about seven levels of worlds linked by a hole under the polestar which forms a tunnel or chute between worlds. But only shamans and kalau can visit these. Claudia's understanding of these worlds was cloudy and she murmured, 'But I'm not exactly sure, I'll have to ask my mother.'

Old people used to have the right to die by asking their eldest son to kill them. The suggestion had to come from the one who wanted to die, being too ill or infirm to continue life. The children would plead with their parent, but if he or she insisted, the son was obliged to carry out orders, usually by stabbing or strangling. But Claudia remembered a man who killed his senile mother at her request thirty years ago and was sent to prison when the Soviet authorities found out.

Roaming around, Valentin and I found a recent cremation with human bones and effects partly covered by newly cut cedar branches, their stems pointing to the sunset. Detours to other bald bits of hillside revealed shoulderblades, thigh bones and reindeer antlers.

On the way back we stopped at the settlement's Christian cemetery. It had only about a dozen graves, most with wooden crosses, the largest decorated with antlers and ribbons. Other wooden crosses had fallen over and were rotting. Only five were named or dated.

Having abandoned my crutches I was limping along using Valentin for occasional support but in a narrow marshy patch my foot sank deep. Freezing water poured over the top into my boot. Valentin pulled me out and we wrung the sock as dry as possible, since wet feet are a quick way to frost-bite.

We came back past the remains of the sacrifice. Ravens cawed with contentment in the trees. The dog's bones and fur had already been picked clean and the head had fallen from its post. Natasha was shocked at the sight.

'The Chukchi are like primitive savages.'

It was the right moment to make ourselves scarce, Natasha had stirred up trouble again flirting with the Little King in front of his Queen, who was now furious with us. So next morning we boarded the big vezdehod along with Vladimir, Yeprintsev, Yvtagin, seven hunters with dogs and guns, also sacks of deer meal, bread, skins, and the usual paraphernalia of sleds, skis and snowshoes.

'Wait, you've forgotten the onions. We can't make fish soup without onions.'

I was hoping to try my hand at deer-herding. First we had a swimming demonstration by a smaller vezdehod we met at the Apuca River. Tracks whirling, it plunged down the bank into the river and thrashed across like a paddle steamer. A vezdehod swims at ten k.p.h.

'The critical thing,' said Vladimir, 'is to enter the current at an angle of twenty-five to thirty degrees. If you head upriver the vezdehod becomes ineffective, it will be swung round and rolled by the current.'

One inexperienced driver had drowned a vezdehod in a calm river, crossing too slowly. 'What he found out,' said Vladimir wryly, 'was that there were several holes in that old vezdehod, so it filled like a sieve and sank, leaving driver and passengers to climb out through the cabin roof port-hole and walk across the ice to safety.' But the vezdehod ahead of us swam well and clawed its way out on to the ice.

Then it was our turn. Our vehicle was tall enough to crawl across on the riverbed without people getting wet, so nose-diving into the water was fun. We got halfway across and climbed on to a sheet of ice, which broke away from the bank under our huge weight and began very gently floating downstream with us on it. A vezdehod isn't threatened by little things like this. Vladimir reversed; the ice-floe tilted again. Then he accelerated, launching us back into the river. We ploughed to the bank, hit it, stalled; backed, charged again, stalled again, but on the third try we made it out on to dry land. Travel by vezdehod is never boring.

The day was a lot colder than the past week. I was chilled wearing two pairs of socks, two pairs of trousers, four layers of tops, scarf, balaclava and fur hat. It was about −20°, perhaps −10° of cold, plus a wind factor of −10° for each ten metres of wind per second. When the sun came out we stopped to fish. Yvtagin lent me a line and one of his table-spoon lures, and suddenly I felt a good tugging and pulled a salmon half a metre long up through the ice-hole. In minutes we were all catching fish, which we roasted on the stony riverside. During our lunch break Vladimir tinkered with a split track iron, and the Little King dozed on top of it. The hunters fished and lazed. Their ex-cavalry guns were date-stamped 1933, 1941, 1943.

It was nine-thirty, sunset, before we located the tabun we had come to visit. Darkness fell about eleven p.m. We were coming up to the time of 'white night' in the north. Our supplies for supper were the remaining fish and some spaghetti, but we had no fork, and each of us had different ideas how to eat it. Two twigs, forked twigs – none was very successful. I crawled backwards to the sleeping-area on a bed of cedar branches, and was lent some extra deerskin trousers and a hat. So the five of us lay in a line in our bags and hats. Only my nose was cold.

Next morning I was going on duty with the herdsmen for the day. We would need two deer-sleds to drive from the yurts to the herd. I drove with Ilcani (can see everything), who gave me Lesson Four: hands lower, and untangle traces as you go. The snow was seldom flat and, at a trot, the sled felt like riding a speedboat, hitting hard waves, riding up and crashing down. It took us an hour to get there and between driving instructions I persuaded Ilcani to tell me about some of the hazards he has survived.

A week ago as he drove his sled out, his deer had seen the main herd, and tried to rush and join it. They swerved across a stony riverbed, flipping the sled on to its side, and eventually forcing him to let go as they charged away, dragging the sled upsidedown, bouncing and splintering. So he had limped back without deer or broken sled to lie groaning over his bruises until the next day when he managed to catch the deer, still in their harness pulling the remains of the sled. He had borrowed another for today. I hoped we would not have a repeat while I was driving.

The deer were jittery and he made me be patient with them. They kept hesitating and looking back, I clicked at them to move on, they obeyed but kept pausing, sometimes to lick snow. There was not much trotting, Ilcani was still bruised. Ilcani is a pure Even, the only non-family member of the brigade. He was born in Achai Vayam, has spent his life tending deer in this region, and is valued for his experience.

We tethered the deer out of sight of the herd, and walked on to find the two herdsmen waiting to go home had kindled a fire to make tea. The men talked briefly about the night, they had found three more dead calves, making a total of fifteen so far. Of the recent deaths, one died of cold, another was killed by a raven pecking its backside, and the last was stillborn. We would check again in the afternoon. In a bad year they may lose fifty per cent of calves to predators, nasty weather, and inattentive mothers; normally it's about a twenty per cent loss.

Our first chores were to locate any stray deer and move the day camp across the hill, since the herd had wandered south in the night to an open valley. The cedar bushes which covered the hill were still full of deer browsing quietly, in no hurry to join the main female herd, with their newborn calves wobbling around. The babes were not afraid of people; Ilcani had to whistle and clap his hands to make them follow their mothers. Two-thirds of the deer had offspring, and we watched one being born, a white one. Ilcani said he did not like white calves because sometimes they are not properly developed. If their jaws are not both the correct length, for example, they will not be able to graze and chew properly. They often kill albinos at birth. When they geld the yearling males they do the white males first, not wanting them to reproduce.

'We choose only the biggest and best male deer for breeding purposes. It's an easy week when they serve the does because the flock stays together mooing and courting. The males hardly eat, they get so thin they can barely stand. But they also begin fighting. One will stand in the middle of the herd and bellow until he finds a rival. Then the herd becomes oblivious to beasts of prey, and we must be extra watchful.'

We spotted one deer without a calf which turned out to be a stray male in the female herd. Every male dream!

On our way we collected antlers. Females shed their horns after calving, the males had already lost theirs, and the old cast-offs are collected for making pantocrin. Ilcani said the herdsmen earn forty-five roubles per kilo of horns. If you find a moose antler you're lucky because they can weigh twenty kilos each.

Mid-afternoon when we checked the herd we found no dead fawns. The second herder, Losher, said the saddle on the next hill was the most dangerous place for the herd, since it was on a wolf path between two basins where the wolves always hunted. Last winter they lost a total of a hundred deer to a pack of nine wolves. 'It's worrying when a fog comes down so thick you can't see the flock, but you can hear or feel that something is wrong. If the herd gets excited they jump around, and young calves are easily squashed.'

His voice was very musical, softer toned than the t-d-k stresses of Chukchi. Eveni originally came from the Habarosk area, and were invaded by the Russians long before Kamchatka and Chukotka. We passed a basin where two years ago they saw a polar bear, and Losher told me a shaggy polar-bear story. The year before a polar bear and its cub had visited Achai Vayam. The mother stayed near the river but the cub ventured into the settlement. An old woman on crutches was hobbling along. She had a big white dog and that day it kept getting in her way, so she hit it with a crutch. From the ensuing snarl she realised it wasn't her dog, it was a polar cub. Passersby said she dropped both her crutches and ran all the way to her hut.

The late afternoon clouded over and became perishing cold as we moved the herd a little more south, whistling and gently encouraging them. By eight p.m. the cold was merciless and the relief had not come, though we had earlier spotted the vezdehod through binoculars sitting on a slope with people-dots working on part of its track. The track must have severed right through because it took three dots about six hours to repair it. One of the dots was our change of duty.

I let Ilcani drive home, we had several steep downslopes to negotiate and my feet were too cold to work as brakes. Also the deer were being tricksy, scenting the female herd and pulling sideways, trying to turn around. The sled slewed and began to tip. We both leaned uphill and jabbed our right feet in the snow to straighten up. The deer jostled, Ilcani cursed them loudly and thumped the rump of the recalcitrant one. It jumped forward and we careered on down. The next hour was a long cold trot along the valley floor.

The following day Yvtagin taught me to use a lasso. He was

organising the counting of the male herd which would begin with a round-up. The Chukchi style of lassoing seemed to be the opposite of the Koryak. You pull a big first loop, then a small one with the end metal ring, then coil in ever decreasing circles. The lasso was supple, made of plaited leather thongs, with a noose end of walrus-hide thongs in a tapering plait for greater accuracy. When a boy is old enough his father usually gives him a lasso. The winter lariat is of skin, the summer one of rope which does not rot in the damp.

Yvtagin explained the different techniques for catching moving deer and a standing one. For still targets you throw the noose high enough to drop over the animal's head, while for moving deer you must throw the loop in front of the animal, so it runs into it. It took me three goes to catch the antler we had put on the ground but I was useless with moving targets.

The male herd, about two hundred strong, was brought down from the hills behind camp in the opposite direction from the female herd, and it congregated near our tents. The herders wanted to catch six race deer. We were a weak force having only four lassoists, plus four others to stop the herd dispersing. They made the herd mill in circles while they discussed which ones to catch.

In order to lasso a specific deer the men divide the herd and make small bunches of deer run between the two groups. Men on either side form a corridor, all trying to lasso the same beast. The first four shots missed, then one lasso looped a white reindeer's neck, the deer fought the rope and it snapped. The herd was growing wild with all the racing to and fro. They trot with such long strides they seem to float above ground. More lassos lashed out as the white one ran with a dark brown deer between groups. One noose caught the dark deer's antlers, but the herdsman knew if he pulled too hard the horns would break off, so with great speed the others threw at the same beast, and one lasso caught its foreleg. When they brought their deer down and put a neck rope on it, they grunted like deer themselves to make it calm. Suddenly a bunch broke away and fled up a valley. Two herders tore after them. The men were doing their share of running today. The remaining herders turned the herd by whistling at it; the deer flowed back, except for a bunch of ten that were racing for the river.

'Get the dog,' someone yelled, and a laika was let off his chain to shoot away and outflank the escapees like any English sheepdog.

Before counting began Yvtagin decided to geld a bunch of undesirable males. One by one they were singled out and two more lariats broke as they pulled taut. It took three men to drop a deer, then two sat on it while Yvtagin performed the initial operation with his teeth. If he used a knife the wound would take longer to heal. Then he squeezed out the testes and twisted them off.

'We can geld a thousand deer in two days,' Yvtagin confided, pausing between nips. 'Though my teeth aren't up to it any more.'

Some geese flew overhead in V-formation. Instantly the herdsmen dropped their lassos and began making honking noises, trying to sound like happy geese having a good feed, to lure those above low enough to shoot at them. But those geese weren't fooled.

The final part of the exercise was to count the deer, by making them move in small groups, as in the round-up, trying to count in fives: I made the total 205, Valentin reckoned 209, and Yvtagin said 217.

At three o'clock we harnessed two pairs of newly caught deer, I would drive one team and Losher the other. We were going to Mirgepin, a one-hut hamlet with a banyo, three hours away. I set off in bad style, cannoning into my escort's sled. The deer tried to bolt, I dug my heels in, my feet hit against something and I bounced in the air, landing on the rear end of the sled, too far back to drive from. I was attempting to slide forwards but both hands were full of reins. I tried to put my feet down again and hop forward but the sled was now going so fast I nearly fell off the back end.

The deer turned sharply, about to have an accident, but fortunately the jolt flung me forward into the driving seat, still with the reins in my hands and the situation was suddenly normal again. For the next hour we went down the valley. My deer were very excited. One was the white one that had broken the first lasso. He was on the right side, the one you control, while the left deer is only for pulling-power. My left one was tawny coloured, young and small, going mad in the harness and pulling like crazy with his head in the air and his mouth open.

The last bit of the journey was great, silky snow, obedient and keen deer, and when they became tired I called to them using the words Lenin had taught me for his dogs, '*Chuar, Omnitza, Periot.*' We were all tired by the time we reached Mirgepin and tethered the deer to graze, but the banyo hut in steam mode was fierce bliss.

Next day I met Kirilov the hunter and he said we could stay at his empty tent back up the reindeer valley. We lived there very happily, working at deer-training with nearby camped herdsmen, and letting life develop a routine of daily excursions driving a sled with whichever deer fell under the lasso. There was also a lot of walking, checking for strays and getting to know the lake-studded hills which led back to an amphitheatre of seven mountains. Usually, walking meant wearing snowshoes. Without them we toiled along, breaking the crust with every step and where streams were running underneath the snow the crust gave way to pockets of air above rushing water. As you drop, the river noise is suddenly loud below. In one three-hour hike above a stream we fell through so often it was intoxicating for the rushes of adrenalin each time the surface collapsed and my feet fell into thin air.

At night I could hear the clicking of hooves as the herd moved around and the barking of dogs at their tethers. Nights were still cold enough to turn the contents of our water bucket to ice and to make any damp clothes go stiff like cardboard. But the plants knew spring was coming and the bushes were beginning to lift their branches, leaving their prints in the snow. I was often aware of the extraordinary quality of sound in the crystalline air, the small sounds of ice slivers skidding away over a frozen river and the almighty crack of breaking ice slabs. There was also the sharpness of outlines, the filigree of melting streams, and the pale green depths of the shadows.

One brilliantly sunny day was perfect for a fishing outing to a nearby lake. Seven of us would take four sleds; a herder called Vasili took his girlfriend and baby. I would drive solo – I doubt anyone trusted my driving. I was given two frisky brown deer, we all jumped on the sleds at the same moment and hurtled off, vying for the lead.

In the soft patches of snow the deer wallowed to their bellies, and you had to brake quickly so the sled didn't run over their backs. In the first hour we had no major stops. My deer wanted to overtake but I kept them back in second place. Things got more hairy as the going got more rugged.

Valodya's sled broke some struts, and my deer fell in such a deep drift I had to call for help to get them out. We covered the kilometres fast. As the land grew hilly, we had to seek ways through the cedar, trotting downhill into a series of basins with ridges between. As we dropped over the last ridge the lake came into view, though we could only see a great flat expanse of snow, ringed with mountains.

Monsters are reputed to live in some lakes of this northern wilderness and one at Lake Chayur is said to have a small head, a long glistening neck, and a dorsal fin, remarkably like its Scottish counterpart in Loch Ness, complete with inconclusive scientific investigations. Sitting beside my ice-hole there were no monsters, and no fish either. To try and reverse our bad luck we made an offering. I gave a sweet and others gave some cotton and matches. Tevlelkot took them to the shore, cut a three-forked twig and lined our offerings up the stem of the twig. He was the only one of us to catch a fish.

The way back was a Grand National of a race, hurdling over cedar branches and ice gulleys for three hours, the only pauses being to help each other back on board after capsizing and getting stuck in waist-deep drifts. I could feel Kungto's deer panting in my ear, their noses on my hat, eager to mow me down until they stumbled in deep snow and cedar brush.

For a while I was in the lead but got overtaken when I slowed in a copse of cedar bushes, their branches had risen above the snow, making springy jumps our sleds bucked their way over. Once clear of the bushes I tried to go faster. The ground dived down a steep bank, which we took at a gallop, hit ruts at the bottom, bounced, skewed and bounced again, still in good style. My main worry was the river looming ahead. All four sleds were in a line, taking the river at speed. The first broke the ice, not too deep. I missed a bunch of high roots, splashed into the water, yelling my reindeer forward and soon they were panting up the bank, wumping over the old grasses and brush where the snow had melted. Next came a side slide, we had to angle our sleds across it by dragging one foot as a rudder. Tevlelkot's sled overturned but he simply bounced up and righted it all in one movement. A last stretch of ice, and the tents were in sight. There was no finishing-line, it was not a serious race, people had stopped to help each other, there were no winners or losers, though for days afterwards I felt exhilarated by that magnificent ride.

The time had come to move the male herd to join up with the females and so we packed up camp. That evening we played lasso the swinging antler which hung from a tall pole. The herders managed one in three. I managed to lasso the man spinning the pole. When the herds were united the counting began again. Yvtagin made it 968.

The calves still looked young and wobbly bounding along,

more were being born every day. I watched a doe with a pair of day-old babies. At first I thought she had twins, but she nudged one towards her udder and forced the other away with her horns. Then she led her own calf away from that spot, leaving the second infant to its fate. For us to touch it would mean its mother would reject it. It sat bleating, so small, it would need to keep bleating loudly for her to find it.

The herd would now begin its long migration to arrive at the coast in two months' time, and I was going back to Achai Vayam with the vezdehod. It was a slow journey, we paused to hunt duck, some of the many geese now migrating past, and a quick red fox which everyone shot at but missed.

8

A Mammoth Hunt

I had heard rumours of deep frozen mammoths being found nearby and my investigation led to an old man who had found a tusk in the region of Achai Vayam fifteen years ago. He claimed it was two and a half metres long and too heavy to carry home, so he had abandoned it along the way. It was never found again. Another man said that when he was five years old he had been with a man who found a tusk by the river. He had brought the tusk to Achai Vayam and exchanged it for vodka. As they say, he drank the ivory.

Our mammoth was reputed to be about thirty kilometres away, in a river cliff beside the confluence of a tributary. According to my map there was a river cliff five kilometres long which fitted with the directions and had a tributary. We would go and camp out there to see what still remained.

Our first effort came to an ignominious end. The horses we had been promised failed to materialise in time. The vezdehod we took instead went down the wrong side of the raging river and did not have enough fuel to swim across. Back to square one. The Little King consoled us with caviar and alcohol, and promised the horses would be at our door next morning at eight a.m. We dined in the best Russian style, and didn't get to bed until three a.m.

I awoke at nine a.m. with a monstrous hangover. The King

was knocking on the front door, Valentin and Natasha were fast asleep. The King suggested he delay the horses until mid-morning. I agreed and went straight back to bed. By mid-morning our hangovers were reduced to dreadful and, watching Valentin, I thought he was still drunk.

The horses arrived again, a feisty bay and a young chestnut for me and Valentin, and a small vezdehod came along to show us where to cross the big river, and to take Natasha and our baggage. When we reached the river Valentin recommended pulling up our waders and he was right. We went in steeply, the water reaching my horse's belly, then his flanks and then halfway up his back. At the main channel we had to wait for a decent gap in the traffic of fast-moving ice slabs, big as cars, jostling in the current, and dodge across quickly to escape them.

The last crossing was deeper but less rapid. After the river the vezdehod developed engine trouble and Sasha the driver had to take it back to the settlement and try to repair it. Smugly, Valentin and I continued with rough directions of the way.

The tundra was occasionally good turf and we cantered along, but much was soggy like walking on sponge. Being permafrost it is always soggy if not frozen. It cannot dry out because it simply draws more melting water up from below.

The stallion was clever at picking his route across the marsh from giant tussock to tussock, ears pricked forward, sniffing and checking where to put his feet. Only once he missed his footing and plunged his chest into a pool. I clung to his thick mane while he scrambled out.

Somehow we got lost in the cedar bushes on top of the cliffs and when we tried to establish where we were from the map, my eyes wouldn't focus and my head ached. So we were greatly relieved when we arrived at the point where the tributary met the river, and found Sasha and Natasha were already down on the shingle beach fishing. Sasha had caught six fish, cooked one for us and made a fire for tea. By this time

I was feeling appalling, with a pounding head, and the thought of tea and fish made me feel ill. But I told myself to belt up, drank the tea, nibbled the food, and began to recover. We pitched our tent on the brink of the cliff with a great view of the river. The wind in the night threatened to blow down the tent but we ignored it and in the morning we felt as good as new.

Where to look? When the surface of the frozen tundra thaws in summer the runoff swells the streams and rivers. Swirling torrents scoop out the banks at every bend, further eroding and undermining the land. Cliffs and south facing headlands crumble a little each summer. As each clod falls, an entombed mammoth gradually approaches the end of cold storage. Centuries can pass between the tip of a tusk piercing the air, and the mammoth becoming visible. We tried the tributary first because we could clearly see three river levels in the cliff, but the ground was hard frozen and we found no recent landslides. Where rocks were not rounded we knew there was no point in looking, an ancient riverbed must have rounded pebbles.

So we tackled the twenty-five-metre cliff just below the confluence. Six metres below the clifftop was a layer of mud which Valentin suggested had settled there when this was the slow-flowing inner part of a bend. The layer below was big pebbles, indicating the river had flowed faster in that period, and any bones would have been pulverised by the action of stones rolling in the current. Hence the silt was our best bet.

Also we needed a place of new landslide because mammoth remains only survive by being deep-frozen in permafrost, and when they finally become exposed and thaw they are eaten by scavengers. The meat is perfectly edible when freshly defrosted.

We laboured on, scanning every stone in another landslide. Siberian legends say that mammoths lived in underground burrows like moles and they tunnelled along with the help of their two long horns. Wasn't it true that they were found under the ground? *Mamont* in Russian means 'earth animal'. They believed the creatures could not endure light or air, and they died when they came to the surface. This was why so many were found emerging from river cliffs, struck by death as they came out of their subterranean kingdom into the light. In regions where earthquakes occur, they were said to be caused by a herd of mammoths tunnelling through the earth at high speed.

'Is this a bone?' said Natasha suddenly, pulling out a pale heavy object the length of my forearm. We grew excited. Moments later I saw an odd yellowish shape which could have been part of a leg bone. Scrambling perilously along the scree, sliding down with every step, it took me fifteen minutes to reach my prize. The measurement from outside to marrow was five centimetres, far too thick for a bear. I stayed there to dig while Valentin and Natasha went ahead.

Yells of delight made me hurry over to Valentin who was uncovering another bone, the largest yet. We scooped it out gently. It was a piece of leg bone half a metre long, weathered and cracked by exposure, but flared at one end like a knuckle or knee, and open to where the marrow had been. Despite its poor condition, I was delighted to have found such proof. The only problem was trying to keep a footing on the crumbling cliff which threatened with every false step to send you sliding down into the fast current below. Over a fish soup supper, we examined our finds: the bones were not fossilised, and were weathered to different degrees, depending on how long they had been exposed to the air. But they were the real thing and could be up to a quarter of a million years old.

Back in Achai Vayam we had supper with the Little King. For

once he talked seriously about his job and his worries about how to market over half the farm's output. A month ago the last Congress in Moscow decreed that state farms may now seek out their own markets. The problem of the prohibitive cost of transport remained unsolved.

Three years ago Yeprintsev had tried to create a canning factory. He had built the shed to house it, and had found an American company who seemed willing to make a joint venture. The necessary equipment was located in America and would cost 250,000 dollars in foreign exchange not roubles. So Yeprintsev had set about making the farm work to supply commodities he could exchange for hard currency, a major item being pantui for pantocrin, which was why he had offered the price for antlers which had led to the desecration of graves on Shaman Mountain. The farm had amassed 50,000 dollars in an international account. At that point new Russian laws froze all such accounts. The money cannot be withdrawn or used; there are no dollars in the treasury; they say Gorbachev used all the foreign exchange on 'look good' policies. The deal with the American company fell through because Russia has no bank guarantees to protect investment. The equipment was boxed and ready for despatch but was never sent.

A group of Russian traders had arrived only that week, Yeprintsev told us. They purchased caviar and furs, but paid in cheap vodka. I had noticed the whole settlement had seemed drunk when I got back. I asked about the chronic lack of roubles to pay herdsmen.

'Oh, that's been so for over a year,' he replied. 'We give them cheques. Quite meaningless, except you can exchange them for goods in the collective shop and the shop can use them to buy supplies. Actual money hardly exists now.'

I was sorry to leave the region where I had enjoyed so many experiences and made many friends. Enough snow had melted to allow a small aeroplane to replace the winter helicopter service. Between the morning's quoted price and eleven a.m when we went to the airstrip, the cost of a ticket had doubled. The pilot saluted good morning, his cap had a naked woman picture as its lining.

Half the plane was reserved for eggs. The seats had been removed and egg-cartons stacked in their place. The Little King gave us a bucketful of caviar when he said goodbye, Vladimir the vezdehod driver gave me a pair of antlers, and Yvtagin gave me his snowshoes.

There were only three other passengers, and the plane took off so steeply that the stacked cartons holding four hundred eggs lurched backwards. We all leaped up as they began to topple, and managed to grab hold of most of the stacks to prevent major losses. But a few eggs broke, making slimy dribbles backwards down the aisle.

My seat was obviously one they'd thought of removing and hadn't, then forgotten to bolt back on to the floor; I was unattached, but fortunately it wasn't a bumpy ride.

'So what's new in Korf?' I asked Tatiana. No scandals, no murders, most of the men were away hunting duck or geese at the beginning of the migration season. I went along to the geology office and museum to look at a mammoth's tusk found locally. It was two metres long but very deteriorated.

Since I was last here the geology unit had cut one hundred and twenty jobs, and would cut more the next week. The shop was closed for the day to cope with another price rise. Tatiana calculated that since I had been in Kamchatka the price of things like bread and matches had risen over one thousand per cent. Sugar, for example, had jumped from sixty-eight kopeks to twelve roubles per kilo.

Tatiana helped me contact the two people I knew in Korf and whom I'd failed to find last time through; they were Pilot Yuri and Valery, the helicopter crew on my Palana music tour three months ago. I was delighted when Tatiana located outrageous Yuri and they all came to the airport to see us off.

I wasn't looking forward to Petropavlovsk and saying goodbye. Natasha had mellowed, I hoped she would find happiness. As for Valentin, he told me, 'You've given me some of the most exciting moments in my life. Without you I would never have known how it feels to ride a galloping horse, and as for that reindeer race! The places we've been and the things we have done, I never thought I'd get to do them and I thank you.'

It transpired that he actually refused to be paid for working for me. I said that was ridiculous, and in the end I spoke to his agents and they said they would spend the money he earned on a new hi-fi set as a present he would certainly enjoy. When I recalled his devoted labour, I was deeply touched.

His next priority as soon as I had left would be to dig his vegetable patch. He was running late and had much to do to make the soil ready. Others were already planting theirs. The roads in Petropavlovsk were clogged with a traffic exodus, roof-racks loaded with wooden posts, raspberry canes and gardening tools. All vehicles that could be persuaded into service were in use. Some had already expired on the road with disconsolate knots of people trying to restart them. Roadside markets had sprung up with instant car-boot sales of plants and seedlings ready for planting out. Spring had begun in earnest.

I stopped in the woods to gather wild garlic for supper, and found some snowdrops, the first flower of the year, a type unique to Kamchatka. Underfoot, nearly all the snow had melted. On the trees, the leaves had begun unfurling. It was time for me to go home.